John Turner

BEYOND THE GOAL LINE

The Quest for Victory in the
Game of Life

God Bless,

Bruce Scifres

Bruce Scifres

INSPIRE POSTERS
INDIANAPOLIS, INDIANA

BEYOND THE GOAL LINE

INSPIRE POSTERS
INDIANAPOLIS, INDIANA

ISBN 0-9728076-2-4

Cover design by Andrew Long / Deep Anchor Graphics
Text design by April Altman Reynolds / Page by Page Design, Inc.

Printed and bound in the United States of America

I would like to thank my wife, Jackie, and my children, Luke, Abby, Caleb and Meggie for their ongoing love and support. They have always been my inspiration and the wind beneath my wings. I would also like to thank Cynthia McMillan for her diligent assistance in typing and correcting the manuscript. Along with Tim Puntarelli, their editing skills helped me sound more eloquent than I actually am. Dennis Stephenson with Hilltop Press and Mike Wadsworth with Redline Graphics were both extremely helpful with the printing of the posters and this book. I would also like to thank Jeannie Schott for her help as a final editor. Jeannie's husband, Dick, has always been one of my heroes. Finally, I would like to thank Mark McGlinchey for helping me get this book started, and for convincing me that I had a story worth telling.

FOREWORD

Soon after the conclusion of our 2004 State Championship season, I was talking with Mark McGlinchey, a friend and
the father of a former Roncalli player. Mark and his son Drew
each had written books, which I had read and enjoyed. In recent
years, several people had suggested that I should write a book
about some pretty amazing things that have occurred during my
time as the head football coach at Roncalli High School. As my
discussion with Mark turned towards this topic, he too began to
convince me that writing a book would be an appropriate thing
for me to do at this stage in my life. With his direction and the
help of his gifted and diligent assistant, Cynthia McMillan, the
early stages of this book were underway.

During my time at Roncalli, I have always considered
myself to be a very ordinary coach who has been blessed to be
surrounded by many extraordinary people. My fellow coaching
staff members, our players and their parents, as well as our school's
administrative team are all part of this group.

It was through the encouragement of friends, former players and their families that the decision was made to write this
book. As such I would like to dedicate this text to the many fine
people who have had such a profound influence over the years
on the great Roncalli football tradition, and who have consequently touched my life in a very special way.

※ ※ ※

I think a high school principal and parents of high school students want much the same thing in their head football coach. They want someone whose influence is such that their children learn lifelong lessons directly related to work ethic, perseverance, positive attitude, team work and resiliency. At Roncalli High School we (principal and parents) also want the coach's influence to have a positive impact on our children's faith and prayer life!

I don't feel overly qualified to comment on Bruce's expertise on play calling, defensive schemes and personnel decisions but I suspect that six state championships means he does those things pretty darn well. I do feel qualified as the principal and the parent of two children in the Rebel football program to say that he does an exemplary job of instilling in the young men who play football at RHS many of the wonderful attributes I listed above.

Our football program under the direction of Coach Scifres is unmatched in terms of living out our school's mission of helping young people learn how to be a light to the world and to grow into all that God wants them to be.

Chuck Weisenbach,
Principal of Roncalli High School
Father of Current Players: Max ('06) and Sam ('08)

❋ ❋ ❋

It has been my pleasure to work regularly with Coach Scifres in his continuing efforts to insure that Roncalli maintains its high profile as the most successful football program in the state of Indiana. Bruce's efforts each fall, along with those of his veteran coaching staff, have been magnificent in their very positive emotional, motivational and performance effect on our football players. These distinctive efforts have resulted in the attainment of six State Football Championships during his coaching career. As well, the mission of Roncalli High School is exemplified in his staff members' faith-based coaching style and substance, with our players being continually reminded that they are important parts of a much greater whole — the Tradition of Roncalli Rebel Football.

Dave Toner,
Alum and Roncalli Athletic Director
Father of Former Player: Chris ('90)

★ ★ ★

In my family, Coach Scifres is more than a preeminent football coach, he has invented a whole new level of coaching prowess that we affectionately refer to as "Bruceball." While "Bruceball" achieves unparalleled winning records on the field, what is most impressive is his ability to bring young men to be people of faith, of conviction, and commitment to follow through in the face of stiff challenges. These are the distinguishing characteristics of "Bruceball" and are what set him apart from all the rest. If a coach, parent, or youth leader want to be distinguished in their ability to lead young people to success, but more importantly, to teach them how they can be successful in life, they need to learn Bruce Scifres' approach to coaching.

Daniel J. Elsener,
President, Marian College
Father of Former Players: Dan ('94),
Andy ('96), Charlie ('04)

★ ★ ★

Bruce Scifres deserves to be recognized as one of the "greats" for the outstanding job he has done for the past fifteen years. Bruce's six State Championships place him at the top among all coaches at any level. A man of deep faith, all areas of his program have prayer as the foundation. What sets him apart from other coaches is that he is most interested in making his players good Christian men.

In the final analysis, the success of a coach can be measured in terms of respect he has earned from his players and his opponents. Honors, won-lost records, championships are all important. But every coach must remember this — he is a living example for all young men in the community in which he coaches. Bruce Scifres has been this example and I salute him for giving all a positive example to live by.

Bob Tully,
Long-time Roncalli Teacher/Coach

※ ※ ※

Throughout my four years at Roncalli, Coach Scifres taught us many lessons about faith, family and football. He always taught us first and foremost that belief in God was number one. With a strong faith in God, everything else in life would fall into place. Always leading by example, Coach Scifres demonstrated a relentless preparation in his pursuit to making us the best Christian men we could be. Whether it was the many hours spent breaking down film or practicing late into the evening under the lights, Coach Scifres instilled in us that we must prepare to be successful. It takes a little more to make a champion. I carried that with me through college and now the real world.

After every game, no matter the outcome, Coach Scifres always told us how proud he was of us. He wouldn't want to be any other place in the world than the Roncalli blockhouse. He cared so deeply about each and every one of us. Even today, almost ten years later, I am truly blessed to still have Coach Scifres as a mentor and teacher. Coach Scifres, thank you for everything you have done for me.

Aaron Irwin,
Co-Captain 1997

Growing up as a young boy on the Southside of Indianapolis, all I ever wanted to be was a Roncalli Rebel Football Player. It was all I ever hoped, dreamed and prayed for. When I finally was blessed with my opportunity to be a Rebel, I quickly realized that I was far more than just another player on a team. I was now a member of the Roncalli Football Family.

What makes Roncalli Football such a blessing is the family tradition of all those who have gone before us. Our father's, uncle's, brother's and cousin's are why there is now a Brotherhood of all generations of Roncalli Football Players.

In this family, Coach Scifres has been a father figure to so many young men. Coach runs a factory of making men out of hopeful young boys. The greatest lesson that I ever learned from coach had nothing to do with football skills, techniques or plays. It rather was a lesson of faith and respect for God and family. Before every game Coach Scifres would remind us that there is no greater way to say "thank you" and honor God, our parents and coaches, and every Rebel brother that has put on the uniform before us, than to give an all out 100% effort and use every ounce of our heart and soul on every play, all night long.

The Roncalli Football Program will never have a down year. This will always be true because our Football Family does not measure success by rings, trophies, or championships. Each and every year is a success when another pack of young men will leave the Rebel Family and take the Christian values which they were taught and lived at Roncalli into the real world.

Coach Scifres, it truly has been a blessing and an honor to know you as a teacher, mentor, coach and lifelong friend. Thank you for all your concern, dedication, effort, faith, hard work, heart, prayer, pride and true love for our Roncalli Football Family. Thank you for being the man that you are and for helping this once hopeful boy become the man that I am today.

Patrick G. Schaub,
Co-Captain 1998

❖ ❖ ❖

Faith, family, school, football: In this exact order, I was a member of the Roncalli High School football family under the direction of one of the best men I have ever known, Bruce Scifres.

The lessons I learned while playing football at Roncalli were great and most of them had little to do with the actual game of football. Coach Scifres never let us forget life was much bigger than the game. Every Friday night after all of our friends and family left the locker room, Coach Scifres would leave us with "do the right thing." Judging by the way he carries himself in all that he does, I think I know exactly what he meant. He meant for us to do the right thing by God. Do the right thing by our family name. Do the right thing for the good of those around us.

He is a better man than he is a football coach, and I do not think there is a better football coach in the state of Indiana. Coach Scifres always did the right thing. He always spoke the truth. He wore his heart on his sleeve. Because of this, he could always walk with his head up. He could look you in the eye when he spoke to you. He would shake your hand with a firm grip. He stands for what is right. He is a good man. He is a great father and husband, and an even better Christian. These are the things I have learned from him. He is a great role model for all people young and old. He is Bruce Scifres and I am proud to call him my coach.

Greg Armbruster,
Co-Captain 1999

❖ ❖ ❖

Roncalli football was never just about winning football games. From day one, we were encouraged to embrace our Christian values and make them a priority. Coach Scifres always taught us to be a good person first, and concentrate on football second.

He reminded us, daily, to always do the right thing, to make our parents proud, and, above all, to welcome God into our lives.

It was truly an honor and a blessing to play football at Roncalli under Coach Scifres.

Chris Eckhart,
Co-Captain 2000

To put into words all the things Coach Scifres and Roncalli Football do for a player is a very difficult task. It is something that can be understood only by someone who has experienced it first hand. Behind all the plays, practices, games and championships, growing boys are shaped into good people as well as young men.

The coaches are very adept at relating football to many things in life, while emphasizing faith, family and education before the sport of football. All players, regardless whether they start, receive the same high quality instruction and contribute to the team equally.

Coach Scifres emphasizes every day the importance of teamwork and preparation for life. He is a master motivator and has played one of the biggest roles in shaping my development as a football player. He is the most humble Christian person I know, and I am thankful for the countless memories he made for my classmates and I the last few years.

Roncalli Football will forever be one of the best experiences of my life, and I am thankful everyday for Coach Scifres and the other coaches, for helping make this game so meaningful and special.

Jason Werner,
Co-Captain 2004
Indiana Mr. Football Award Winner

※ ※ ※

I like to think that I am a part of the Roncalli Football Tradition even though my playing days took place over forty years ago as a Sacred Heart Spartan. I have watched the Roncalli football program over the years — many of those years as a Dad of three sons who played the game; many more of those years simply as a fan; a booster; an alum.

I know first hand how football can teach life's lessons. But mix in the devotion to and expression of faith in God, love of family and one another, and loyalty to the school community and the end product is going to be a good citizen, a hardworking family man who understands the value of sacrifice, has respect for authority and believes that individual accomplishments are for the greater good of the team, the community and the family.

I have great admiration and respect for Bruce Scifres. Not only because he knows how to produce champions on the football field but also because he, like so many others at Roncalli has had such a major role in preparing young people to be solid citizens in our community.

On behalf of the many other former players that claim a part of this great tradition, I want to thank you, Bruce, for what you do. The championships were fun, the memories are great but, most importantly, thanks for helping our sons grow up to be good Christian young men.

Chick Lauck,
Member of the 1966
Notre Dame National Championship Team
Father of Former Players: Kevin ('87),
David ('93), and Brian ('94)

※ ※ ※

It has been my distinct pleasure to have been acquainted with Bruce Scifres for the past twenty-two years. I've gained a genuine admiration for the qualities of this man during the past decade as he has coached two of my sons.

Coach Scifres has an approach which deals with standards that are faith-based and without compromise. He has created a true "family" atmosphere in his professional life. While his accolades as a football coach are many, his "sphere of influence" has left an impact on hundreds of young men who've played and successfully moved forward in all walks of life.

I could put it best by saying Bruce Scifres has risen in his profession to a level which has few peers and few critics. He is a player's coach, a parent's coach and, without question, a man of impeccable integrity and character!

Frank Sergi,
Former Head Football Coach and Athletic Director
Father of Former Players: Mark ('00) and Tim ('04)

※ ※ ※

During football season, my wife and I joked that we could stop parenting our son Taylor for a few months. Coach Scifres and his staff do such an outstanding job with the kids on the team, and it shows in their attitudes, academics and on-field performance. I have always maintained that if my kid never saw a down, and if the team never won a game, I would insist that he be a part of the Roncalli football program.

While I am not quite sure how Coach Scifres turns these scrawny kids into fine young men, whatever he does is powerful. Clearly, his belief in God and his insistence on being mentally and spiritually prepared translates to football skills, football wins and football championships.

Strip away the football success and every year this program prepares nearly a hundred kids for life. The football success is the icing on an already incredible cake.

Jeff Donnell,
Father of Former Player: Taylor ('04)

⊠ ⊠ ⊠

Bruce Scifres is a wonderful football coach but he is so much more than a coach to my family and me. He's a Christian man with a heart that swells with his love for Jesus Christ and for the young men who play Roncalli Rebel football.

In June 2002, my husband died after a 14-month battle with cancer. He was a loving husband and father of four children. Five weeks after my husband's death my son, Philip, began his varsity football season as a sophomore at Roncalli. The next three years of high school were filled with many challenges, both on and off the football field. Coach Scifres was the "Dad" that he so desperately missed and needed. He was there to guide, support and share these memories with Phil. He always made himself available to my son as he struggled to grow and mature during these difficult years.

As a mother, I can never adequately thank Bruce Scifres for supporting me, for his love and his kindness. I want to take this opportunity to congratulate him for all of his accomplishments on the football field, but more importantly, I want to thank him for being a living example of Jesus Christ everyday to my son and to all of the young men at Roncalli.

Robin Andrews,
Wife of Former Player: Karl ('79)
Mother of Former Players: Nick ('99) and Phil ('04)

⊠ ⊠ ⊠

The ultimate compliment we can pay as parents to Bruce Scifres is simply to say our sons and nephews learned more about their faith, their religion and Christian behavior from him and the Roncalli football program than they did from any religion class taken at Roncalli High School (… and I make that comment with the highest respect for our religion curriculum and teachers.)

Humility, respect and love of God and family are at the forefront of his beliefs and his behavior. He is the epitome of the gentle giant and certainly is worthy of the title "gentle man." It is very rare for such a physically huge man and highly successful coach to not only be such a humble person but also to command humility from his players. Bruce does that … he walks the walk.

Whether you came in as a cocky or shy freshman; whether you became the name-dropping all state running back; or the no-name lineman, one thing is for sure … you will leave Roncalli football a more humble human being. You will not only be coached in football but also humility, honesty, integrity and life by one of football's greats and by one of life's masters — Bruce Scifres.

Now that this generation of Schembra and Nalley boys have finished playing football, it is very apparent the reasons they chose to play are not nearly as important or life-molding as the lessons they learned from Coach Scifres and the RHS football program. What they did on the field as players is such a small part of who they became and what they strived for as a result of Bruce and his "life lessons." It seems trite to say that he goes above and beyond the duties of a coach. He genuinely cares about every player and he cares about what they become after Roncalli football. He is a great role model as a coach, father and husband.

It is not trite but rather the heartfelt truth when you know these sons and nephews repeat how respectfully and lovingly he speaks of his wife and kids. It is not trite but truthful when you know his heart broke for my young nephew whose father was dying. It is the heartfelt truth when you know that a son chose this man to stand on the altar with him on his wedding day.

He makes life-long impressions on impressionable young men. Many come back and stand next to the man who so rightly prepped them for life. They proudly stand with the huge man who casts a huge shadow: a shadow of trust, kindness, humility, love and faith. He stands for what is right in the world. It is our belief that boys stand a little taller after standing with Bruce Scifres. We are blessed for having him as a part of all our lives.

Kathy Nalley-Schembra,
One of Indiana's All-Time Winningest Volleyball Coaches
Sister of Former Player: Dick Nalley ('72)
Mother of Former Players: Sean ('97) and Tommy ('99)
Aunt of Former Players: Richie Nalley ('00)
and Marcus Nalley ('02)

CHAPTER 1

New Beginnings

Throughout my life I have been blessed with many amazing opportunities — both personally and professionally. With those opportunities, I have developed a pretty good ability to adapt to new circumstances and environments. As I entered my thirties, I saw my personal life coming together exactly as I had envisioned it. However, in my professional life, although I was happy, it seemed I had not quite found my place in the world or a job that felt like "home." As a high school teacher and coach, I was still looking for that perfect school.

Whether consciously or subconsciously, I think this nagging feeling had prompted several of the moves I made between schools over the years. The funny thing was that I wasn't necessarily unhappy in any of those positions. It was simply a case of feeling that when I found the right spot I would know it — and everything would just click right into place.

Towards the end of 1989, the realization began to dawn on me that without knowing it, I had actually found my career "home" early on. After completing my Master's degree, I spent three years as a teacher and assistant coach at Roncalli High School in Indianapolis. It was ironic that in order to appreciate this amazing environment I had to leave for a time and see what else was out there. As I became increasingly aware of my need to return to Roncalli, I began to actively pursue my options and my timing could not have been better. As fate would have it, Roncalli's head football coach at that time was in the midst of leaving the coaching profession to pursue a career in the business world. I quickly "threw my name in the hat" and began to work my way through the selection process.

On February 6, 1990, my wife Jackie and I had just returned from dinner to celebrate my thirty-third birthday when the phone rang. Pat Cox, the principal at Roncalli High School, was on the line. I had recently interviewed for the head football coach position at Roncalli. Although other coaches who had applied may have been more qualified, I felt like my interview had come across as sincere. It also seemed that I fit within the guidelines of what they were looking for. The fact that I knew four out of the five members of the selection committee before interviewing did not hurt my chances either. Pat informed me that the selection committee had made their decision and wanted to offer me the position.

Although she gave me the option of taking a few days to think it over, I quickly accepted. I knew this was where I needed to be; taking more time was not necessary.

I was already quite familiar with Roncalli. I had taught there seven years earlier, from 1980 – 1983, as a U.S. History and Geography teacher. I was also an assistant varsity football coach as well as the Head Track Coach. I left Roncalli, a Catholic school on the Southside of Indianapolis, to teach in the public school system for seven years. During that decade, Roncalli won two State Championships in football and already had a very well established tradition in place. I knew I would be taking a pay cut to leave the public school setting to go back to a parochial school but my previous time there showed me that Roncalli was a very special place.

At the time, the coed school had about 700 students in grades nine through twelve. As a Catholic institution, the faith-based mission of the school made the discipline and overall daily atmosphere very attractive. Each day began with school-wide prayer, the Pledge of Allegiance and many teachers began every class with a prayer or reflection. The students wear a modest school uniform. Many of the faculty and staff have been there for many years and are completely committed to the Christ-centered mission of the school. Many of the finest people I have ever met in my life are teachers at Roncalli.

The fact that families are paying a substantial amount of money each year to send their children to Roncalli works wonders when a teacher calls home to inform parents that their son or daughter is not behaving or turning in weekly assignments. Parent involvement and support is outstanding throughout the community. As I was celebrating my thirty-third birthday, I was at a point in my professional career where all of these characteristics were more important to me than the money I would be sacrificing to make the move. Becoming the head football coach at Roncalli was just icing on the cake.

That night, I had trouble falling asleep. I reflected on my unconventional start in athletics. The fact that I had never played an organized sport prior to eighth grade was a direct result of my upbringing. I was from a large family — there were eight kids born within a time span of eleven years. My older brothers, Sam and Kim, were seven and five years my senior respectively. I was born fifth and in the middle of five girls — two older and three younger. We lived out in the country several miles from school. None of my older siblings had played organized sports. My mother and father both had full time jobs to support our family. Often times, my mother worked evenings and my father worked overtime to raise eight kids. Consequently, transportation was a problem.

There were, however, neighborhood sports where competitiveness and aggression existed. My brother Kim had his front teeth knocked loose during a backyard football game and, after the ensuing medical bills, football was no longer allowed for my brothers and me. Dad said so. Case closed!

The inability to play organized school sports was very frustrating since I was always one of the biggest, tallest and fastest kids in my class. The fact that I was the youngest of three boys and my older brothers were unusually adept at keeping a steady supply of knots on my head, I was also probably one of the meanest kids in my class. (Just for the record, some of those knots were well deserved, others were not.) I always thought football would have been the perfect solution. Alas, my frustration.

Through grade school and early junior high, I was somewhat shy and awkward, and would probably have been considered a bit of a country bumpkin. My size precluded me from ever being bullied, but I was certainly not a member of the "in" crowd. I always hoped athletics would be an avenue for me to gain the positive recognition that almost all teenagers crave. At that time, I had no idea of the tremendous impact athletics would ultimately have on my life.

The summer before my eighth grade year, I had a grand idea. The decree was clear: no football. But my desire to play would not ebb. I would have to play without my parent's consent. Luckily, I had a friend who lived about a mile down the road who was going out for eighth grade football. I told my parents I was going to be a manager for the team and that I would catch a ride home with my buddy each night so they wouldn't have to worry about picking me up. I then forged my father's signature on the athletic physical form. I told my friend's mom that our washing machine was broken — hoping that she would volunteer to wash my practice uniform. She unwittingly obliged. I am not proud that by the eighth grade, it appeared I had become an accomplished liar. Sam and Kim were the only people who knew my secret. I told them just in case an emergency arose or something of the sort. They agreed and actually delighted in my deceit under the premise that I would take all of the blame (and my father's wrath) if I were caught.

Even though they were excited for me, I think they were also perturbed that they had not been allowed to play the sport we all loved. Sam stood 6' 4" and had always been one of the toughest kids at Plainfield. As a senior in 1968, the turmoil our country was going through was reflected in Sam's demeanor. Getting into fights at the drop of a hat wasn't unusual for Sam. One time, when I was in the fifth grade, I was riding in his car and noticed a heavy set of chains under the seat. When I asked what they were for, he replied, "Just in case I need them." Even at that age, I figured out what that meant and didn't ask any more questions. Needless to say, with his size and mindset, he had the makings of a great football player.

Kim, on the other hand, was a little easier going. He was also tall — about 6' 3" — was fast and had great hand-eye coordination. He has always been an exceptional athlete but, unfortunately, never had a chance to play either high school or college athletics. I have absolutely no doubt he would have been an outstanding football player, and would have excelled in other sports as well.

By the time I was in eighth grade, both of my brothers had graduated and moved out on their own. I'm sure this aided their decision to help me carry out the deception of playing football without my parents' consent. With their encouragement, my "illustrious" athletic career began.

Since I had never played organized football before, the coaches started me at tackle on offense and free safety on defense. They knew I was one of the fastest players on the team but, due to my size and inexperience, they felt I should start out on the line.

The first time I touched the ball in an organized contest was in the third game of the season on a tackle eligible play. This was a crafty play where the offensive tackle was eligible for a pass. That first pass reception went about 60 yards for a score. From that moment on, I was moved to running back, a position I would occupy for the rest of my career. In the remaining games, I carried the ball a lot and was able to score several touchdowns. It didn't take long for my sisters to figure out what was going on through the school newspaper. They skillfully used this information to blackmail me into taking care of their household chores — taking out the trash, washing dishes, etc. They knew I would do anything to keep my parents from discovering my secret. Outright fear was a real motivating factor.

The source of this fear was a powerful 6' 2", 270 lbs. man named Duane Scifres. And I wasn't the only one afraid. So were most of the kids in the neighborhood and my older brothers too! The thought of my deceit (and his discovery of it) followed by a sharp blow to the head ... well ... it kept me up at night. Other than occasional, well-deserved spankings, my father was never abusive to me. However, I had never told a lie of this magnitude nor had I ever forged his signature. It was this fear of retribution that led me to carry out my sisters' chores dutifully.

I was able to make it through eighth grade football without my parents finding out. Furthermore, my busy schedule in the fall working as a "team manager" for the football team seemed to break the ice with my parents. After that, they agreed to allow me to join both the basketball and track teams.

The summer before my freshman year, my brothers and I decided to "come clean" with my parents about my participation in football. With my brothers at my side to lend moral support, and to do most of the talking, we sat down with Mom and Dad to convince them to allow me to openly play football in high school. Despite the fact that we had all banded together to deceive them throughout the previous fall football season, they took the news very well and weren't as angry as I had feared they would be. (We left out the signature forging, though. No sense in taking further chances.) Regardless, my brothers were able to eloquently plead my case and persuade Mom and Dad that I had a talent for football that could lead me to receive a scholarship and allow me to attend college. Since no one in our family had ever attended college, the enticement was appealing and they gave their consent.

I continued to play all three sports throughout my four years at Plainfield High School. As much as my life had felt unfulfilled and frustrating through seventh grade, the opposite was true after the eighth grade. My involvement in athletics changed my life for the better almost immediately. My self-esteem skyrocketed as I acquired a new identity as an athlete. I was good at something and was beginning to receive some of the positive recognition all teens yearn for. I was named President of our freshman class and even though I still felt very much like a tall dork around girls, I think for the most part I was well liked in my school. As a junior and senior, I became a little more adept socially and I truly enjoyed my high school years. The success I had in athletics was in no small measure responsible for the growth in my confidence and new found purpose in life.

I was a two year starter on the varsity basketball team and, during track season, set our school record in both the shot put and discus. As my brothers predicted, I was also blessed to receive a football scholarship to Butler University in Indianapolis.

Looking back on my days at Plainfield High School, I have many fond memories of teachers and coaches who guided me and influenced my life in a very positive way. As I prepared to enter college, I believe the seed was already planted that someday teaching and coaching was a career I would embrace. My experience with the fine educators at my high school certainly influenced that thought process.

As I began my career at Butler University, I was proud to be enrolled at a school with a great academic reputation. Being able to play football made it even better. I immediately joined a fraternity house and ended up being a roommate with Bob Casselman, who had been a former archrival from Brownsburg High School. Since both Plainfield and Brownsburg are in Hendricks county, about ten miles west of Indianapolis, the rivalry was intense. Bob was a year older than I and a good athlete. We both started at center for our respective basketball teams and guarded each other in some heated, elbow-slinging battles. Bob stood 6' 5", weighed about 220 lbs. and was one of the leading scorers in the area. As I was 6' 2" and about 200 lbs., guarding him was a real challenge. Without question, he was a better basketball player than I was (although I have never given him the satisfaction of stating that to his face.) In spite of his abilities, however, we beat them in basketball his senior year and he did not play a great game. (I have, in fact, given myself the satisfaction of stating this to his face on numerous occasions.) Thank goodness he has a good sense of humor. As he and I both played football at Butler and were roommates, we became great friends. Living in a fraternity provided ample opportunity for social activity. Suffice it to say, we had a lot of fun. With the exception of my first semester, I was on the Dean's list each succeeding semester of my tenure.

In football, my first chance to start in a collegiate game was midway through my sophomore year. In this first start at tailback, I rushed for 206 yards on 42 carries. At the time, both of these statistics were school records. Before graduating, I was able to set a couple more rushing records as well. Many times, I would carry the ball over 30 times a game. Despite the fact that after those games I felt like someone had beaten me with a baseball bat, I loved every second of it. The accomplishment I was most proud of, beyond any records or awards I may have received while at Butler, was the fact that I never took myself out of a game. In my mind, giving someone the satisfaction of knowing they had hurt me was completely unacceptable. Perhaps, the countless knots my older brothers had so generously placed on my head earlier in life paid off in this regard. Developing mental toughness and the ability to fight through pain and adversity is one of the first lessons an athlete must learn. Regardless of how talented an athlete might be, until they have mastered this concept, they will always struggle with mediocrity. This is one of the "lifetime lessons" I will discuss later.

Through my college career, the toughest opponent I encountered was Dick Nalley, who was two years older and the starting tailback for Indiana Central University — Butler's archrival. At 5' 10", Dick was a solid ball of muscle. As he was a senior and I was a sophomore, he was clearly the better running back. Although we beat them that year, I was in awe of him as an athlete and tremendous competitor. At the time, I had no idea that twenty-five years later at Roncalli, our lives would once again become entwined.

My days at Butler were probably the most fun and carefree years of my life. I made great friends and was blessed to receive a great education. Upon graduation in 1979, Bill Sylvester, the head football coach at Butler, asked if I would become a graduate assistant coach for him. After my senior year, I received the Hilton U. Brown Mental Attitude Award — the highest award given to a Butler athlete. I guess Coach Sylvester thought I had the potential to be a good coach and an asset to the program. The fact that I was an education major made it even better. The year I spent as a G.A. allowed me to almost complete my Master's degree and gave me the opportunity to coach at the collegiate level for a year. This position also allowed me to coach with Bill Kuntz, who was an assistant at Butler at that time. In the fall of 1980, Bill was named head football coach at Roncalli, and asked if I would come teach and coach with him. My initiation at Roncalli had begun.

I stayed at Roncalli for three years under Bill Kuntz and then, in 1983, I moved south for a year and taught high school Social Studies in Brownstown, a small community about fifteen miles west of Seymour, Indiana. At the time, I was dating Jackie Reinhart, who later became my wife. The fact that she lived in Seymour weighed into my decision to move south. In addition, I wanted to get a feel for life in southern Indiana. By now Jackie and I had been dating for a couple of years and I knew she wanted to stay in southern Indiana. I used this time as kind of an experiment to see if I could be happy living in this rural environment.

I enjoyed my year in Brownstown and met some wonderful people. Yet that spring, when an opportunity presented itself to move back to Indianapolis to teach and coach at Lawrence

Central, a large public high school on the east side of Indianapolis, I was excited about the possibilities. There were about 1600 students in the school. It had great facilities, a wealth of athletic talent and included a pay increase. My duties involved teaching Social Studies, assistant football coach and head track coach. The school had a well-established track program and I knew I would be coaching some of the fastest kids in the state. Though reluctant at first, Jackie finally gave her blessing for me to move back to Indianapolis.

In my six years with Lawrence Central, both the football and track programs produced several Division One caliber athletes. In the spring of 1990, on the heels of my acceptance of the Roncalli offer, our track team finished runner's up at the state track meet. Our top sprinter, Ron Brown, won both the 100 and 200 meter dashes in that meet, and our 400 relay team became state champs as well.

I had made some very close friends while at Lawrence Central. Yet, in spite of the pay cut I would be taking and the fact that I would be leaving some very good people behind, I was anxious to begin my career as Roncalli's head football coach. In my time as a public school educator, I had really grown to miss the discipline and Christ-centered atmosphere of the parochial school setting. On my thirty-third birthday, I had no doubt that God was opening a door and calling me back to Roncalli. I was excited about answering His call.

Back in the day. This is me taking a handoff in a game at
Butler University.

CHAPTER 2

Creating A Philosophy

There is an old saying in the coaching world that "You coach the way you were coached." I think there is a lot of truth to this. If you played for a coach who yelled and screamed a lot or if your coach cussed a lot or used negative reinforcement to "tick you off" in order to "motivate" you, then you will probably be inclined to use these same methods to "motivate" your players. Likewise, if you played for a coach with a calmer demeanor or someone who was very skilled at positive reinforcement, you will probably model these traits for your players.

I would say the majority of the coaches I played for leaned more toward the calm, controlled demeanor and relied more on the positive reinforcement approach. Consequently, I would say most young men who have played for me would say this is usually my coaching style as well. This is not to say that on occasion I do not become agitated and vocal. There have certainly been times where I have yelled and screamed with the best of them. However, this is not my normal coaching style.

Since they do not hear it from me very often, when I do raise my voice or become agitated, the players are usually very attentive. This can be a very effective teaching tool. I firmly believe, however, that you will "always draw more bees with honey than with vinegar." When I was playing, this approach was definitely more appealing to me, so I certainly try to conduct myself in this manner.

My coaching philosophy has certainly been shaped by the outstanding mentors I played for, as well as the head coaches I have had the opportunity to coach under as an assistant. Kermit Davis was the head football coach at Plainfield High School during my time there. He had come from Ohio during my junior high days, and very quickly established himself as an innovative proponent of the "run and shoot" offense. In the early 1970's, at least in the state of Indiana, this offense was new, exciting, explosive and hard to defend.

The fall of 1971, my freshman season, Coach Davis led the mighty Plainfield Quakers to an undefeated 10-0 varsity season. Unfortunately, the playoff system was still two years away in our state, so this team did not have a chance to contend for a State Championship. However, I am confident they would have been very competitive.

During my sophomore year, I was able to play a lot at fullback, and then as a junior and senior, I was a halfback where I was able to both carry the ball and get downfield for passes. We finished my senior year at 8-2, losing our last game in triple overtime to Speedway. This loss kept us out of the playoffs and even though my senior season ended in disappointing fashion, I thoroughly enjoyed playing for Coach Davis. He was very good at creating number advantages through motion and misdirection.

Another innovation he introduced was the two-platoon system, where everyone only played on one side of the ball. Although I really would have liked to have played some defense, this did allow us to use time very efficiently in practice, and probably cut back on injuries to key players. It also allowed each side of the ball to develop an intense sense of pride as a unit. On game days, the offensive starters wore their jerseys along with blue berets to school, while the defensive players wore their jerseys and red berets. At first it seemed a little goofy to be wearing berets around school, but eventually it became a source of pride and honor to have earned this right, and the rest of the student body responded appropriately. Kermit Davis eventually retired as one of the all-time winningest coaches in the state of Indiana. I have always admired and appreciated his innovative approach to coaching.

One of his assistants, Dave Teany, was the defensive coordinator and the staff "crazy man." He was also our head track coach. Coach Teany had graduated from Danville High School, another Hendricks county rival, and many tales had been passed down over the years about his exploits — both on and off the playing field. When Coach Teany got mad, everyone, coaches and players alike, steered a wide path around him. In addition to his intense pride and competitive spirit, he had a wonderful sense of humor and was an excellent motivator. I distinctly remember him pulling me aside one day during my sophomore year after I had gotten in trouble in a class for acting foolish. To this day I can remember his exact words, "It is your destiny to have your name remembered around here for many years to come. Right now, you are at a turning point in your life. Do you want to be remembered as a clown or idiot who had talent but let it all go to waste? Or, do you want to be remembered as someone who used his God-given talents to the best of his ability to make a positive name for himself? The decision is yours!" That was it. He didn't yell at me or threaten to beat me or demean me in any way. Those words made a lasting impression on me. I'm sure I was not perfect during my last two years of high school, but I do know I became more focused and a better student because of his burning questions. Quite frankly, I have used these same words with a handful of young men over the years who I felt were not very focused or were not making good decisions. These questions have burned in their hearts and have had a similar motivating appeal. Even as a middle-aged man now, it is still good for me to reflect on these words from time to time.

I was blessed to have several good men for coaches during my days at Plainfield High School. This good fortune continued during the next four years at Butler University. Bill Sylvester was Butler's head football coach. He had been the starting quarterback at Butler in the late 1940's. After several years coaching high school football at Catholic schools in Indianapolis, he went back to Butler as an assistant in 1964 and became the head coach in 1970. Being a graduate and long-time coach in the Catholic school system, his coaching style was certainly a reflection of this background. Coach Sylvester brought a strong element of spirituality to the way he ran the program. To this day, I still have nothing but respect for Bill Sylvester. I have always admired his integrity and ethical approach to athletics. He emphasized that we should always work hard and do everything we could, within the rules of the game, to win. He was a knowledgeable strategist, and led the school to numerous conference championships. He was a loving father with several children at home. His oldest son, Bill Jr., would later come to Butler to play for him. Bill Jr. went on to be my predecessor as the head football coach at Roncalli, where he led the school to its second State Championship in 1988.

Coach Sylvester has always been a great example of a loving father and husband. Now that I am married, with children of my own, I appreciate this quality more than ever. Looking back, what I have always admired most about my college coach was the way he incorporated a spiritual approach to the game of football. There's no doubt the game is one of the most violent in the world of sports and, therefore, a deep irony exists in that some of the best and most aggressive players are at the same time very spiritual and highly religious. I first began to understand this under Coach Sylvester.

Although he never tried to force his spirituality upon us, there was never any doubt by the way he conducted himself that he was a man of devout Christian faith. During my time at Butler, I never heard him swear; and you will find the use of foul language is quite common on other collegiate sidelines. Every Saturday afternoon before we would take the field, he would lead the team in prayer. There were two common phrases he used during prayer that I have adopted as part of my pre-game message over the years. The first was "Help me to remember, Lord, that nothing is going to happen today that you and I together can't handle." The second, and the one I have used most often, is "Please grant us strength and courage to play like men in your eyes." I would always feel a tingle run down my spine each time he would ask for this blessing. It was very important to me that I do everything in my power to hold up my part of the bargain. I was honor-bound to give my best to God and this man who humbly interceded for this strength.

I guess what I always respected most about Coach Sylvester was his decision to be a good Christian role model for a bunch of college athletes. I doubt it was mandated by his contract, it was simply a choice he made each day. I recently had an opportunity to tell him publicly, among a group of about 100 former Butler football players, that, next to my father, he had a greater positive influence on me than any other adult male in my life. He played a major role in my decision to ultimately become a teacher and a coach. With all of the other former players in the room that day, I told him he would never be able to measure the positive influence he has had on all of our lives. I asked for a show of hands to see who in the room had coached a sport of some sort at any level. Almost every man in the room raised a hand. I then asked how many in the room had caught themselves saying or doing something that Coach Sylvester said or did when he was coaching us in an effort to have a positive impact on young peoples' lives. Again, almost every hand in the room went up. I finished by telling Coach that his influence did not end with those in attendance that day, but was being passed on for generations to come. I was glad I had an opportunity to thank him in this way. It was truly an honor to play for a man of his character.

After finishing my year as G.A. at Butler, I began my career as a high school coach as an assistant under Bill Kuntz at Roncalli. Like me, he had both played for and coached under

Bill Sylvester, and consequently brought the same integrity and character with him. It's clear I started my high school coaching career at the right time and place, because integrity and ethics were the hallmark of Bill Kuntz's program in the early 1980's. He had attended Cathedral High School, an Indianapolis Catholic school rich with tradition, prior to playing at Butler. He was familiar with the Christ-centered environment a Catholic school provides. Coming from a public school, this was an interesting experience for me. Although at that time I was not Catholic, I had been raised in a Christian household. It was both educational and inspirational for me to experience the Catholic school atmosphere.

Bill proved to be a master at motivating young people and making them feel good about being involved in a wholesome activity like football. I was immediately impressed with the ease with which he shared his faith in God with the players and how eagerly they responded. This parochial environment was certainly new to me, but I felt immediately drawn in. At first, I was concerned with how I might be received in the program and at the school, due to my non-Catholic heritage. But everyone in the Roncalli community was very welcoming and non-judgmental. I was grateful for this acceptance since it made me feel comfortable very early on.

I believe Bill Kuntz was the perfect mentor under whom to begin my high school coaching career. He led Roncalli to its first football state championship in 1985, two years after I had departed to give the public school setting a try. Bill's younger brother, Joe, was the starting quarterback on that team. I know that was a very special experience for both of them.

As mentioned previously, I left Roncalli in 1983 and spent the next seven years in the public school system. Six of those years were at Lawrence Central High School, a large county school on the east side of Indianapolis. The first five years I worked under head coach Bob Ashworth. He was from southern Indiana and had played four years in the Big Ten at North-western University. Bob's father, George Ashworth, had been a long-time and very successful high school football coach. As one might expect from a coach's son, Bob was excellent with the X's and O's, and was strategically very sound. An exceptionally bright man, Bob taught most of the advanced classes in the Social Studies department. Since I was also in this department, I had an opportunity to see first hand Bob's expertise with teenagers. Lawrence Central had a significant minority population and Bob's skill at promoting interracial harmony was outstanding. He had a knack for showing interest in the players' families and lives outside of football. As a former Big Ten lineman, Bob was a large and intimidating man, which often came in handy in regard to enforcing policies both in school and on the field. He had also assembled an outstanding assistant coaching staff. Two fellow assistants, Frank Sergi and Bob Hasty, each celebrated the birth of sons during my time with them at Lawrence Central. In fact, I distinctly remember when Tim Sergi and Andrew Hasty were born. Just a year earlier, Coach Ashworth's oldest son, Nate, had been born. Since Jackie and I had not yet started our family, it was fun to watch these three toddlers roaming around the sidelines and interacting with the players. It was also good for me to witness these three men being devoted fathers. I suppose the irony continues. I had no way of knowing that one day all three of these families would re-enter my life and these three toddlers in particular would play invaluable roles for Roncalli and my own family — even insofar as being pivotal for the creation of this very book ... but that story will come later on.

Prior to the '89 – '90 school year, Bob Ashworth announced he and his family would be moving to Kansas. His wife, Beth, was a heart surgeon and would be taking a new position there. Bob also found a head coaching position at a good-sized school around Wichita. With his departure, Frank Sergi and I were the top two candidates for the position of head coach. I felt I was ready. I had been a loyal assistant and my junior varsity teams had posted stellar records. It certainly seemed I was ready to be a head varsity coach. However, ultimately, Frank was offered the job and although I was upset at first, in retrospect, it was a good decision and eventually worked out for the best. Frank had been loyal also, had been the dean of students and was as steady and dependable as anyone I ever met. He was meticulously organized — something I have never been. I have heard it said before that "a messy desk is a sign of genius." If this is true, one glance at my desk would be a clear indication that I could give Einstein a real run for his money! However, what I lacked in organizational skills, I made up for in motivational abilities. Looking back on it now, the year I spent coaching under Frank Sergi proved to be a blessing. I have never met anyone who is more honest, works harder or has more integrity than Frank. He was a great role model and I learned a great deal from him. Since he and I were friends, I worked hard that season to be a loyal assistant. This proved to be a good experience for me since I would become the head coach at Roncalli the next year.

Each of the head coaches I played for and coached under have had an impact on my current coaching philosophy. Three men that had been assistants with me during my first stint at Roncalli were also positive influences — both then and now. Joe Hollowell was the defensive coordinator in the early 1980's under Bill Kuntz. He was a great coach and one of the most intelligent I have known. In the spring of 1990, shortly after I was hired as head football coach, Joe became the new principal at Roncalli. I have now known him for over twenty-five years, and admire both his devout faith and his strong sense of family. He and his wife, Diane, have eleven children, and my wife and I have always been amazed at how respectful and well-behaved their children are. Their first five children were boys and I have had the honor of coaching all of them during my time at Roncalli. All five have great attitudes, tremendous work ethics, fine leadership skills and more than their share of mental toughness. Consequently, they have all been fine football players. I'm sure it is a source of personal pride to Joe that two of his sons are currently working towards becoming priests. And, there is little doubt that they come by their faith honestly. Joe Hollowell is a faithful man who loves his family and has devoted his twenty-eight years as an educator to Roncalli High School. I am confident this has played a huge role in the type of adults his children are becoming. In recent years, he has become the President of Roncalli — the public school equivalent of a superintendent. Chuck Weisenbach, a solid Christian leader who shares many of Joe's fine qualities, has replaced him as principal. As an alumni of the school, Chuck loves Roncalli and the students who attend it. In the same tradition as Joe's boys, Chuck's two sons are currently on the football team as well.

Likewise, the oldest son of Dave Toner, our Athletic Director, played for us back in 1990. Dave is an alumni of the school and a wonderful administrator under whom to work. The fact that I have coached the sons of our President, Principal and A.D., and I still have a job, indicates to me that they like what we are doing in the football program. Furthermore, it is a blessing to have administrators who understand and appreciate the value of athletics and who support what we are trying to do. They all agree the primary purpose of the school is to provide a faith-based education for every student who attends Roncalli. They also acknowledge and support the fact that athletics and other extracurricular activities are a vital part of the process. Again, I feel blessed to work with and for administrators who share this belief system.

Bob Tully, another assistant coach I had worked with before at Roncalli, has also had a profound influence on my coaching career. The school opened in 1962, the same year Bob began his career as an educator. He actually lived in the school the first couple of years and has been a permanent fixture ever since. Referred to affectionately as "Mr. Roncalli," Bob has held practically every job imaginable during his tenure. Though he stands only 5' 6" tall, nobody has a bigger heart or is more well loved than Mr. Tully. As a long-time religion teacher, he has provided a strong Christian influence on literally thousands of lives, including my own. As an assistant football coach, his knowledge of the game and boundless energy make him a valuable asset to the program. Every kid that graduates from Roncalli loves Bob Tully … as I do.

The third person who coached at Roncalli when I was there before, and who is still there today, is Tim Puntarelli. He is our Dean of Students, and coaches our quarterbacks. Since we met in 1980, Tim has been one of my best friends. As a Notre Dame graduate and religion teacher — and since he has a few more years in education under his belt — I have always valued Tim as a mentor. I have relied on his levelheaded approach to life on numerous occasions to help keep me from saying or doing something brash or stupid. I have been very blessed that he has always been a loyal friend.

Each of the gentlemen I have mentioned in this chapter have been a profound, positive influence in my life. In some way, they have all helped to shape my philosophy as a coach as well as my philosophy of life. I would like to share some of this philosophy in this chapter.

I have grown to believe that every coach has two primary jobs. The first, and the lesser of the two, is to teach young adults how to play a game. Every coach wants to teach his kids how to run faster, jump higher, throw and kick better, etc. In the same vein, it is certainly a coach's job to teach the rules and strategies of the game. These things are important, but I firmly believe the second task is far more important and also more difficult.

The main job of a coach is to teach his players how to live their lives, and how to be the kind of person God wants them to be. I believe this all starts with the priorities of a program. If the priorities are in the right place, I firmly believe winning will take care of itself. Even very early in my career, I felt we needed four priorities or standards for which we want all of our athletes to strive:

First and foremost, we want our players' involvement in football to strengthen their faith relationship with God. As a parochial school, we have an obligation to make this their top priority. To this end, we have player-led prayer after every practice and game. Every Thursday night, we have "senior scripture," when a senior shares a bible verse with the team and then explains how it applies to his life or the football program. He then hangs the verse inside his locker.

Second, we want our players to be good people. We want them to love and honor their parents, and they should be respectful to teachers and people in authority. As our players graduate, we want them to be good citizens and productive members of society. Ultimately, we want them to be faithful husbands and loving fathers to their children.

Third, we expect each player to make the most of the wonderful opportunity they've been given to receive a great education. Most parents make tremendous financial sacrifices to send their children to Roncalli and we expect the students to do their part. We emphasize that only one Roncalli football player has gone on to be drafted into the NFL. In the spring of 2004, Nate Lawrie, a Yale graduate, was drafted in the sixth round by the Tampa Bay Buccaneers. Quite obviously, the odds of becoming a professional athlete are miniscule. Therefore, education is of the utmost importance. Our players know that if they do not behave in school or if they fail to keep their grades up in the classroom, they will not stay on the team for long.

Finally, our last priority for our athletes is that we want them to be good football players. We certainly work them hard and demand their utmost effort at all times. However, I think every young man in our program understands that winning football games is not the most important thing we do. At the same time, I firmly believe if the first three priorities are in place, winning football games will take care of itself.

This philosophy is the culmination of the many lessons I have learned from the great men I have played for and coached under as an assistant coach and it has served our program well over the years. More importantly though, I believe it has served our players well by teaching them valuable lessons about life and faith.

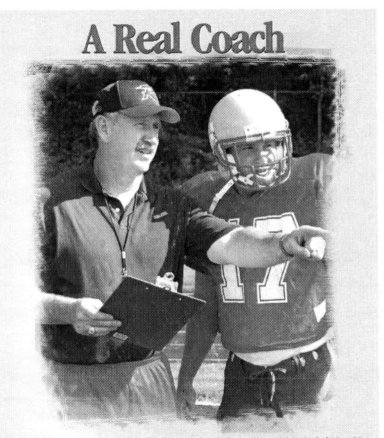

A Real Coach

A REAL COACH knows that his primary responsibility is not to teach the mechanics of his sport, but rather the fundamentals of life. He prioritizes sportsmanship, and teaches his athletes to maintain integrity and class in victory or defeat. He instills honesty and a sense of fair play. His athletes learn the merits of hard work and enthusiasm as they observe him model these traits each day. He teaches them to be thankful for their abilities and to always do their best to utilize their gifts. His athletes learn to never give up in the face of adversity, and that their attitude is the only thing in life they have complete control over.

A REAL COACH knows that his ultimate goal is not to win championships or individual accolades. Instead, it is to teach a boy to become a man. He understands the only scoreboard that really matters is the one in his heart. For it is here that he sees the score that counts most... HOW MANY LIVES HE HAS TOUCHED AND CHANGED FOR THE BETTER. This is where a real coach finds his greatest reward.

CHAPTER 3

Season of Turmoil

It is a common belief that a coach's success should not be judged before his fourth season at a school. By this time, his seniors have spent four years in the program and his system should be completely in place. Even though I felt I had a sound coaching philosophy as my foundation, the job I did as a coach during my first four years left a lot to be desired. Like most assistant coaches, I had always been confident that when I became a head coach, I would be able to combine all the best qualities of each coach I had played for or coached under, and would be an immediate success. I quickly found out it doesn't quite work that way. In the fall of 1990, my first season as a head coach, we had a very talented group of seniors. Chris Toner, our current Athletic Director's son, was an All-State linebacker. Brian Sanders, an All-State defensive end, also rushed for over 1,000 yards as our starting tailback. John Roeder, who later returned to help coach our freshman team, was an All-State tackle. We also had several other outstanding players in a senior class of sixteen. The sixteen players in our junior class were scrappy, yet exceptionally small and we only had ten sophomores come out that first year. I have never quite figured this out — since it was my first season and I hadn't had the chance to tick anyone off yet. As a result, we started the season with forty-two players.

My first game as a head coach was against the mighty Franklin Central Flashes, a neighboring southside school.

Franklin Central had been the elite football program in the state during the 1980's and was coached by Chuck Stephens, one of the best ever in Indiana. In the early 1980s, they had won three consecutive state championships and were State Runners Up a couple of times later in the decade. As luck would have it, Chuck's 1990 team was rumored to be his best ever ... what a way to begin my coaching career!

We played them very close for three quarters, then they began to pull away. One of Chuck's best players on the 1990 team was his son, Charlie, who went on to have an outstanding collegiate career at Purdue. After defeating Roncalli in the first game of the season, the Flashes went on to have a perfect 14-0 record, which was topped off by a 4A State Championship. The way I saw it, if you had to lose your first game as a head coach, losing to a team of this caliber made it a little easier to swallow. After his perfect 1990 season, Coach Stephens retired, and I still have nothing but respect for him as a coach and as a person.

Since we had started the season with only forty-two players, injuries had cut that number to thirty-six by tournament time. One of those losses was Brian Sanders, our starting tailback. The smaller our numbers got, the harder it was to keep kids healthy. We were desperately beat up as we hobbled into the playoffs. We lost the second game of the tournament to finish the season with a 6-4 record. It was a disappointing finish for our seniors who had been a part of a state championship team during their sophomore season. However, it was a great learning experience for me as a new head coach. It made me aware of two critical issues in high school football — strength and numbers.

Heading into the 1991 season, we knew we had some seriously undersized seniors and only ten returning juniors. Thankfully, our incoming sophomore class was very talented. Although they struggled through a 4-3 freshman season, they had a nice blend of size and speed. In the end, we finished the year 6-5, which would certainly be considered sub par by Roncalli standards, but we thought it was a wonderful season. When it came to getting the kids to play hard, keep great attitudes and simply have fun, it was one of the best coaching jobs our staff has ever done. One of the senior captains from that team, Ray Shelburn, is currently a religion teacher at Roncalli and coaches our linebackers. Pound for pound, he was one of the most tenacious players we have ever had and has now become a vital part of our current staff.

As the 1992 season began, the class of ten players were now our seniors and we had some good players in this group. Matt Evans, the quarterback, probably had the best natural throwing motion and arm of any quarterback I have coached. He threw for well over 1,000 yards that season. It was also exciting to watch the progress of our junior class since they ultimately occupied most of the starting positions. We ended up having a very good 6-3 season. Two of those losses were to a highly competitive Chatard team — the second loss was a heartbreaker in the tournament. After three seasons, my record as a head coach was fairly unimpressive (18 wins, 12 losses.) My fourth year was still on the horizon.

Naturally, there was a lot of anticipation as we started the 1993 season. The talented underclassmen we had relied on so heavily the previous season were now seniors and we were returning our entire starting offensive line. I think any offensive coach would agree that this is the best place to have experienced players coming back. They were good-sized kids who were all smart, tough and very athletic. Many of our best players were also back on the defensive side of the ball. As athletically gifted as this senior class was, the thing that excited our coaching staff the most was the "chemistry" of the senior group. They were very close knit with great personalities and an extremely competitive nature.

At the beginning of the season, we lived up to these high expectations by steamrolling our first four opponents by a combined score of 114-6, and we finished the regular season 8-0 — without really being challenged. After outscoring our first two sectional opponents 76-18, we faced an undefeated Zionsville team in the sectional championship game. Ironically, I had a dream that week that the game would go into overtime. Afterwards, I had trouble falling back to sleep so I got up in the middle of the night, went to my office and pre-scripted in exact order what we would run if the game went into overtime. The next day, we practiced these plays in order with the understanding that this was our overtime script. I think some of the players thought I was crazy because we hadn't had any real challengers all season.

As fate would have it, the weather was horrendous on game day. By the time the game started, the temperature had fallen considerably and, during the game, we periodically experienced torrential downpours. All in all, playing conditions were miserable. My premonition a couple of nights earlier was accurate. After battling back and forth, regulation time ended with the score tied at 21 points each. Mike Bohn, our tailback, had put forth a Herculean effort to keep us in the game. At 5'11" and around 170 lbs., his courage and determination were amazing. We lost the coin toss prior to overtime, which meant we would have the ball first on the ten yard line and only four downs to score. The team followed the overtime script we had practiced exactly, and we punched it into the end zone and kicked the PAT. Zionsville answered with a screen pass that went in for a score. They opted to kick the PAT to send the game into a second overtime.

Per the rules, they were on offense first in the second overtime period. On third down, their quarterback, an excellent scrambler, rolled to his left and, under pressure, fired the ball across the middle and into the end zone. Craig Cothron, our free safety, came out of nowhere to make a diving interception. Our crowd, who had packed the visitor's bleachers and were standing several deep along the fence line, erupted into a deafening roar. It was our ball on the ten yard line going in.

Continuing to follow the overtime script, we called a power

toss left with Mike Bohn carrying the ball. He had already carried the ball about forty times, and was battered and exhausted. In spite of his fatigue, I knew he already had way too much invested in the game, and his senior season, to ever surrender. As he ran to his left, the Zionsville outside linebacker flew past our kick out block and smashed into Mike for what should have been a three yard loss. Somehow, Bohnie bounced and spun his way out of the tackle and weaved his way across the final ten yards, diving into the end zone for the game winning score. Almost immediately, hundreds of Roncalli's faithful fans swarmed onto the field and engulfed the mound of Roncalli players who had jumped on top of Mike in the end zone. It was a tremendous on-field celebration.

I learned two very valuable lessons from this game. First, never take an opponent for granted. Second, always pre-chart your course of action in the event that overtime presents itself. Time and time again, I have found that these decisions must be made in advance — based on what you have seen on film when your head is clear and you aren't under mind boggling pressure, which muddles thoughts. Ever since the 1993 Zionsville game, I always pre-script an overtime sheet — regardless of the record of the upcoming opponent. Prior to each game, the team and I thoroughly discuss and practice each play of the script. In my fifteen years as head coach, we have had ten games that went into overtime and have won eight of them. Beyond the shadow of a doubt, our overtime scripts have served us well!

After the Zionsville battle, we played very well in a decisive 37-0 Regional win. The following week, as we were preparing for the Semi-State game, our school received some crushing news. The father of Jason Simmons, one of our co-captains, passed away unexpectedly. Jason was a three year starter and one of our best linemen. The loss of his father was personally devastating. Al Simmons had been very active in the CYO youth sports program on the south side. He was very well known and much loved. His sudden death stunned our community. Despite the emotional stress and tremendous sense of loss, Jason did what he felt his father would have wanted him to do. He played an emotional and inspired game to help lead us to a 42-0 Semi-State win. Players and coaches alike wore black wrist bands with the initials A.S. to honor Al.

With a strong sense of duty and loyalty to Jason and his family, we began to prepare for the State Championship game. Our opponent was Northwood, who was also undefeated that season. We received word that their senior class had never lost a game as seventh, eighth, or ninth graders. The community of Northwood believed their team, like ours, was on the road to fulfilling their destiny. We knew they would be the toughest opponent we had faced all year.

Surprisingly, Roncalli took the opening kickoff and marched the length of the field and scored on its first possession. In the second quarter, we again mounted a long, clock-consuming drive to make the score 14-0 at the half. Mike Bohn had 178 yards rushing on 23 carries, and our defense had done a superb job of containing their potent option-oriented offense. Given that our team had performed so well up to this point, we felt pretty good going in at the half with what we thought was a pretty decent lead. Our feelings would change abruptly in the second half.

In the third quarter, both our offense and defense began to struggle. Northwood's aggressive and emotional play had a lot to do with that! Since we were protecting our lead, our offense was not going to take any unnecessary risks, and we were forced into some three-and-outs. Northwood's option game started to click as they began to eat up the clock with sustained drives. They scored in the third quarter, but missed the PAT kick. Midway through the fourth quarter, they scored again and left Roncalli holding a narrow 14-12 lead as they lined up for a 2-point attempt. It was a well-designed option play to the left. After the pitch, it was two on one as the tailback and lead blocker were approaching our right cornerback. Brent Carver, all 5' 9",

165 lbs. of him, was our starting quarterback and right corner. He somehow knifed outside the fullback and made a diving shoe-string tackle on the tailback, who otherwise would have walked into the end zone. We knew we had narrowly held our 14-12 lead as we mounted a drive deep into Northwood's territory. Unexpectedly, Carver threw a play action pass for a touchdown to Jason Jaffe, our flanker. Unfortunately, we were called for holding, and after the penalty yards were assessed, we were unable to score. Northwood put together one last drive in the final two minutes of the game and fought their way to our 30 yard line. With one second on the clock, Craig Cothron made another huge interception at the goal line to end the game. We had won Roncalli's third State Championship as a school — and my first as a coach!

Our 14-0 record that season was truly a wonderful tribute to our players, who had worked so hard and had been so committed to each other and the program. Mike Bohn finished the season as the state's leading scorer and rusher — he had 3,165 total rushing yards for the year. Not only was this a new Indiana single season record, the total also made him the leading rusher in the nation for the 1993 season. He was later selected as runner-up for the Mr. Football Award, the honor given to the top player in the state.

All in all, we couldn't have asked for a better senior class. They gave us everything they had and were excellent leaders. In many respects, this should have been one of the best seasons I could ever ask for as a coach. Unfortunately, it was not. As hard as our coaches tried to hide it, I think many of our players knew there were some profound problems among the coaching staff. The problems began in 1990 when I was hired as head coach. Before I returned to Roncalli, the staff had been a very young, successful and tight-knit group. In the end, the top two finalists for the position of head coach had been one of the existing assistants and me. After I was awarded the position, I found there was still some resentment among the staff that their fellow assistant hadn't gotten the job. The assistant promptly found another head coaching position and left Roncalli. Since then, he has had much success and has proven his coaching ability with three State Championship seasons at that school. Since that time, I have gotten to know him. He is a great guy and a very talented coach and I wish him continued success.

During my first four years as head coach, we had a very definite split right down the middle of our staff. Using political terms, I will refer to these two sides as the "Old Guard" and the "Left Wing." The Old Guard consisted of myself, Tim Puntarelli and Bob Tully. This was essentially the group who had coached together ten years prior. The Left Wing had come later and were younger. On the eight man staff, I would say three were definite left wingers, and the remaining two swung back and forth. When I was hired, it was made perfectly clear to me that being good Christian role models for our players was by far the most important job our staff faced. It was my job as the head coach to make sure everyone on staff followed this mandate.

Quite frankly, I did not do a very good job of it. I tried to make it very clear that as a Catholic school, there should be no cursing by either players or coaches. Yet, a couple of coaches would frequently swear in front of the players. After a while, when I tried to crack down on this, one assistant began passing out weekly "scouting reports" with acronyms on the cover sheet in which some of the letters represented cuss words. This same assistant even implemented a policy where every time our defense came up with an interception, the player would shout one of these acronyms as a signal for everyone else to block for them. Of course, at first I had no idea what they were saying, or what these "secret" acronyms stood for. I think many of our players thought it was pretty neat that they had a secret code between them and a young assistant, while the "old fogey" head coach didn't realize his "Old Guard" rule was being broken. I finally pulled aside an upperclassman that I trusted and got the scoop. I then put an end to this little "game."

Our school has always had a strict drug and alcohol policy for athletes, and tobacco products are part of this policy. In my second year as head coach, we had to kick one of our best senior players off the team for smoking. Since most of the Left Wing had significant chewing tobacco habits, I received a handful of phone calls and letters from parents about the double standard on our staff because we had coaches using tobacco in front of the kids. When I talked to our Principal about what I should do, he said, "That's simple. Just tell your coaches not to chew in front of the players." I wish it would have been that easy. In spite of the warnings, a couple of coaches continued to chew in front of certain players, and word was getting around that they were allowing the players to chew as well. Although it was just hearsay, I felt caught in the middle. Should I let it go or deal with it? If the rumors were true, they could be fired on the spot. Or, I could just sit back and do nothing about it. Needless to say, there was an ongoing war between the Old Guard and the Left Wing. Sometimes the factions would begin arguing with each other in front of the players, which is breaking the "Cardinal Rule" of a good coaching staff.

They say you should never point the finger of blame at someone else, because you will always have three fingers pointing right back at you. Having said this, I am going to point the finger of blame. I deserve the blame for whatever uneasiness and difficulty this season brought. What should have been one of the best seasons of my coaching career actually turned out to be anxiety-ridden and miserable.

Again, I want to restate that it had nothing to do with the players, their attitudes or their efforts. The seniors on the '93 team were outstanding, and were just a reflection of the leadership they received from their coaches. As the head coach, it was my responsibility to be a better leader for our assistants. Since then I have figured out that any good head coach or manager must do three or four things to be a good leader:

☞ Make expectations clear.

☞ Make consequences equally clear.

☞ Communicate immediately when guidelines are not followed.

☞ Hold all employees accountable when they choose not to abide by the rules.

I had not done a very good job with any of these steps; the blame fell squarely on me.

After the '93 season, by the spring of '94, most of the Left Wing loyalists had moved on to other schools. However, probably the best liked and most respected of the Left Wing was still on staff. That spring, four of the other five assistants said they were going to resign if the coaching staff remained unchanged. The stress, argumentation and cover up was too unnatural and we all knew where the problem was. They didn't want to be a part of a staff that was constantly at war, and their intent to quit proved it. Likewise, I had no desire to ever go through another season of such turmoil and knew the full responsibility of resolving this issue fell squarely on my shoulders.

Therefore, at the end of the '93 – '94 school year, I fired the final member of the Left Wing. I knew there would be strong repercussions with this decision. Among our graduating seniors, he was probably the most loved and respected coach on our staff. I knew there would be many misinformed people who would think he was fired because of his popularity or as a result of jealousy from the rest of the staff. Trying to remain as professional as possible under the circumstances, I was very judicious about speaking of this issue. The administration and people who really needed to know the facts were given the details. I thought this was the most professional way to handle it.

The downside to this was that rumors were rampant, and in the eyes of many in the Roncalli community, I had done a foolish thing, brought on by professional jealousy. The fact that I was unwilling to discuss the details with people probably made matters worse. That summer was miserable because I felt like I was unable to defend myself. The good news was that the people whose opinions mattered most to me — the rest of the coaching staff — were absolutely supportive and were excited about the possibility of us creating a cohesive, unified, loyal staff where everyone got along and actually liked each other. What started out being the toughest and most troublesome decision I have ever made in my career ultimately proved to be the best decision I have ever made. As far as our staff was concerned, we were heading in the right direction. With all the senior talent that was graduating from the '93 team, we knew we would have to have complete unity among our staff to have a shot at defending our state title the next season. Though we had resolved some issues heading into the summer of '94, we all knew some major obstacles lurked on the horizon.

CHAPTER 4

Back-To-Back

I love football. I always have and I always will. I believe the game of football is a microcosm of the game of life. There's hard work and rewards; setbacks and success; determination, courage, loyalty, fighting for a common cause and an endless list of other "lifetime lessons" to be learned on a daily basis. Perhaps what I have grown to respect the most about football is that, just like life, at the very core of success is human relationships. I firmly believe that a team with mediocre talent and great chemistry has a better chance of performing "when the chips are down" than a very talented team with mediocre chemistry. Of course, I am biased, but I believe the very nature of the game makes this concept more true in football than almost any other sport or endeavor a young man might pursue.

Since there are twenty-two positions in football, there are numerous roles and assignments that must be filled. A young man can lack speed, height, jumping ability and hand-eye coordination but still become an excellent football player. As long as a player works hard, understands his role and does his best to do his job every second of the game, he has a good shot at being successful. Knute Rockne once said, "I play not my eleven best, but my best eleven that think as one."

We use the phrase "the Roncalli football family" quite frequently. I have used the following analogy at various times when I have spoken at coaches clinics. It is perhaps a bit barbaric, but

I think it proves a very good point. Imagine that you are at a gathering with friends, and someone informs the group that there is a 6' 5", 315 lb. behemoth outside who is furious because someone has backed into his new Porsche. He needs to take out his frustration on someone, and has invited the guilty party to step outside and fight him. Most people, unless highly intoxicated, would not volunteer for this detail. However, if someone informed you that this same beast was outside and had your parents, spouse and kids preparing to beat them all severely if you didn't come out to fight him, would your reaction be different? Obviously, and without hesitation, most people would sacrifice their own health and safety to protect their loved ones. This is the concept behind the loyalty and brotherhood of a "football family." In my years as a coach, I have learned the stronger the sense of family among our team, the more inclined that group is to play with courage and emotion when faced with adversity, and the less likely they are to surrender.

Heading into the 1994 season, we had some "family issues" that needed tending. Since I had just fired a very popular assistant coach, our players had the entire summer to listen to misinformed members of the community ask, "What in the world is going on with that football program?" I had two primary objectives to fulfill that summer before the season began. The first, and most pressing, was to name a new defensive coordinator. The older and more experienced coaches of the staff declined the opportunity. They knew very well that the D-coordinator would have to put in an immense amount of time breaking down film, charting offensive formations, plays and tendencies of each upcoming opponent. In light of these duties, it was also not a job to dole out to a young and inexperienced coach. I knew I would probably have to hire someone from the outside. After dealing with the crisis in '93, I resolved to make all hiring decisions with loyalty as the top criteria for the rest of my coaching career. Early in the summer, I bumped into an old high school buddy named Phil Gatts. I had played football and basketball

BEYOND THE GOAL LINE

with Phil in junior high and high school, and he was also an outstanding pitcher for the baseball team. He was an excellent athlete and a very intense competitor. As a cornerback on defense, Phil was famous for his "clothesline" tackles and his very aggressive and borderline insane play. Phil and I had a common bond as he had an older brother, Bob, who, like my older brothers, regularly administered beatings ... in the name of "family love" of course. I have no doubt this played a role in the formation of Phil's reputation as a very physical and punishing football player.

My brothers owned two pairs of boxing gloves. As high school knuckleheads, a group would gather at a friend's garage for tournaments. Phil and I would usually end up in the finals. Since I was a little bigger and stronger at the time, I was able to maintain my title of "heavyweight champion of the world." However, Phil was my greatest and most difficult competitor (our heads may have been mixed with the same cement.) It was through these wars that Phil and I forged our friendship, the depth of which was about to enter a new era.

After high school, Phil received a scholarship to play defensive back at Indiana Central University, Butler's archrival. Coincidentally, this also made him a teammate of Dick Nalley's. So, our battles continued during our four years of college, with us seeking each other out on the gridiron for head-to-head contact whenever possible while not letting our rivalry interfere with our assignments on the field. Attempting to run Phil over was slightly akin to the boxing ... and those games remain to this day some of my favorite memories of my time at Butler.

Several years after we had gotten out of school, Phil's father, an ex-marine, passed away. I remember going to the funeral and being amazed at how composed Phil was. I had always known he was a very strong-willed person. The family was seated in the first row and as the mourners began to file past the casket, I paused to shake Phil's hand and extend my condolences. He stood, gave me a big bear hug and began to sob uninhibitedly. I was proud that I could offer comfort to my old friend as he gave his father back to God.

When Phil and I bumped into each other early in the summer of 1994, he told me that he was now coaching freshman football at Mooresville High School, a town just south of where he and I grew up. His wife, Ann, who had also been his high school sweetheart, was from Mooresville. For several years, Phil was a varsity assistant at the school, but had recently asked to be moved down to the freshman level so he could coach his own team. He told me he missed varsity football. Since loyalty was a top requirement for my newly formed coaching staff, and since I have never met a more loyal person that Phil Gatts, it seemed like the perfect match. I was overcome with a feeling of relief that I had accomplished my first objective — to hire a defensive coordinator who would work hard and be loyal to me and the rest of the staff.

The second objective for the summer was to unify the returning players into a cohesive group and convince them that in spite of the previous coaching staff problems, we were now going to be stronger than ever. Our staff decided that to help the healing process, we were going to hold our first ever "Rebelympics." To promote team unity, we divided the young men into groups of three with a sophomore, junior and senior in each. These three partners would compete against the other groups in a series of mostly silly events, followed by an overnight "sleepover" on the game field. The competition included a tug of war, egg toss, Frisbee competition and the ever popular bat-spin relay.

Phil's in-laws own a funeral home in Mooresville, and he was able to procure a couple of body bags for a special competition. One member of each team would climb into the bag, then his partners would zip it up and carry him 30 yards. The process was repeated two more times and all three guys had a chance to be carried in the body bag.

Our final competition was the egg drop, which took place

at the back of the stadium. One player, usually the senior, climbed to the top of the bleachers with an egg in his hand. One of his partners, usually the sophomore, would lie on his back on the ground with his head near the base of the bleachers and an up-turned cup just below his neck. It was the job of the of the senior to crack his egg and try to drop as much of the egg as possible into the cup waiting below. It was obvious some of the seniors made little to no effort to hit the cup, and for the sophomores, it certainly added a whole new perspective to having "egg on their face" — but it was a success. We all laughed over and over and each silly event brought some normality back to the squad. We liked each other and they liked us. More importantly, our players got to see the mischievous and fun-loving side of Phil Gatts. They fell in love with him from the get-go. On Phil's behalf, those feelings were mutual.

Since we started the Rebelympics at 10:00 that night, we were into the early hours of the next morning when our last event ended. Our last order of business as a group was to turn off the stadium lights for some reflections by the coaches and a couple of former players.

After that, I pulled the seniors aside, and gave them each a sheet of paper and a pen. I then asked them to find a spot on their own where they could write down some thoughts about what Roncalli football meant to them and why it was special. I also informed them that I would be putting their letters in a "time capsule," which I was going to bury somewhere on the school grounds to be dug up in a few years by a future team. With this in mind, I asked them to write their thoughts as if they were writing a letter to a future player. As our seniors scattered and began writing, I could see several players swiping at tears as they wrote to future Rebels. Several players even came back to me and asked for more paper to finish their thoughts.

When they were finished, I placed their letters in a plastic container and wrote the name of each senior on the outside. I decided to bury the container a few days later. I wanted to be the only person on the face of the Earth to know where the time capsule was.

Although our last activity of the evening was finished, most of the guys weren't ready to go to sleep. Many of them just wanted to hang out and talk, which I gladly took part in. A few continued to play games and as they ran on the field in the moonlight, I took a few moments to revel in the thought that my second objective of the summer had been accomplished. The players had grown closer and I was able to get them to accept and embrace Phil as their defensive coordinator. The start of a new season loomed before us.

Our upcoming senior class may have been a little above average as far as overall athletic ability, but the junior class was actually more talented. We had very few returning starters from the previous year's championship team, but the senior class provided some great leaders. At the end of two-a-days, the team selected four captains. One was Rick Scott, a big tight end who would later get a full scholarship to Toledo. Another was Jeremy Stahley who, at 5' 10" and 165 lbs, was one of the best inside linebackers we have ever had. The third captain was Trevor Wilson, who had set our all time record for most pounds lifted and would go on to win our Mental Attitude Award for the year. The fourth captain was Brian Lauck, who would start for us as both quarterback and free safety. At season's end, Brian was selected as our offensive MVP and was without question one of the most intense competitors I have ever coached. Brian is now a pharmaceutical salesman and our varsity defensive backs coach. He brings the same fire and competitive energy he had as a player to practice each day as a coach. We are blessed to still have him as part of our program.

The 1994 season opened against a very good Franklin Central team. We had pounded them the year before and they returned the favor by beating us 23-0. Since Brian was our only senior starter in the backfield, I was concerned after the opener that we might have trouble moving the ball or putting points on the board. I was mistaken. We beat our next five opponents by a combined score of 164-46. We entered week seven, our homecoming game, facing Scecina, an undefeated eastside Catholic school. For the first half of the game, it was a hard-fought battle. However, in the third quarter, Scecina began to make some things happen and scored a couple of times to take control of the game. In front of a huge homecoming crowd, it was like all of the wind had been taken out of our sails. With our heads hanging, we more or less surrendered in the fourth quarter. Scecina beat us that night 28-7. Certainly, we had lost games at Roncalli before, but I had never seen one of our teams just lay down and die before — especially not in front of a huge homecoming crowd like that.

We had just started a traveling trophy with Scecina that year, a nice, life-sized brass football on a base to go to the winning team's school until the following year. They had won it fair and square. But, to add salt to the wound, the next night at Roncalli's homecoming dance in our gymnasium, a few Scecina players arrived with a tiny replica of the trophy — like you might find at a dollar store. They presented it to our Principal, Joe Hollowell, when he stopped them at the door. They told him since we couldn't win the real trophy, they wanted to present us with a runner-up trophy. Joe accepted the award and watched them walk away with noticeable smirks on their faces.

There were two things these young men didn't realize when they made the presentation to Joe. The first was that Joe was a Scecina graduate, and still had strong ties to the school. The second, and more importantly, was the rich football tradition that courses through Joe's veins. Mojo Hollowell, Joe's father, retired as one of the all-time winningest coaches in the state of Kentucky. As I mentioned in Chapter Two, Joe was the defensive coordinator at Roncalli when I was there as an assistant in the early 1980's. He was an outstanding football coach, one of the best I have ever been around, and a tremendous motivator. Although they did not know it at the time, their presentation to

Joe Hollowell was probably the best thing they could have done for our football team.

The next Monday, during school, Joe asked if he could address the team before we left the locker room for practice. Joe certainly had the contacts at Scecina where he could have called them and gotten their players in trouble. But he had a much better plan in mind. As our players were all seated around him in the locker room, he asked our four captains to stand up. He began to address the team by saying, "You know, I have been at Roncalli now for about fifteen years. During that time, I have grown to love and respect Roncalli football and everything it represents. What I have always loved most is the fire and passion that our players have in their heart. I have seen Roncalli teams lose a few games over the years, but I have never, ever seen a Roncalli team quit! The other night, in front of a huge homecoming crowd, I saw this team just give in and quit! Now, I'm sure by now you have heard that some Scecina boys were at the dance on Saturday night and asked if I would make this presentation to you guys. So, on behalf of Scecina High School, I would like to present the first annual runners-up trophy to the captains of this team!"

Joe held the trophy out to Jeremy Stahley, who was the captain standing closest to him. Jeremy, whose father had been a standout linebacker at Roncalli in the early 1970's, was an extremely proud young man. In fact, he played with as much heart and passion as any player in the school's history. For several seconds, he simply stood there looking at the miniature trophy being presented to him. From where I was standing, I could see his eyes welling up with tears. After a few awkward moments, he began to slowly shake his head no and backed away. Joe, always the master of motivation, pointed the trophy in the direction of Brian Lauck and continued with just a slight taunting tone in his voice, "Well, come on now. You guys earned this trophy. You deserve it. So, the least you can do is accept it." Brian, who was just as proud as Jeremy, turned away from the trophy with his head down. I could see a tear tracing down his cheek. It seemed our captains weren't going to budge, but neither was Joe.

After several more awkward moments, I stepped forward and said, "Mr. Hollowell, thank you for this presentation. We all know it was well deserved and I know right where this trophy belongs." I placed it on top of the big screen TV, which was a prominent location usually reserved for our tournament championship trophies. I proceeded to inform the team that the trophy was to stay there for the rest of the season. Furthermore, it would remain there through the next season until the Monday after the Scecina game. I gave strict orders that no one was to touch it or damage it in any way. As directed, it remained there and it served its purpose throughout the rest of the season.

The next Friday night was the last game of the regular season. It was also a home game and Senior-Parent night — where all of the seniors were introduced with their parents on the field before the game. Our seniors are always charged up emotionally for this game. Combined with the embarrassment of homecoming the week before, I almost felt sorry for our opponent. That night, and in the first game of the playoffs the following week, we outscored our opponents 108-14. The team began playing like they had something to prove. However, we knew the next few weeks would be different since we would have to defeat some outstanding teams in order to advance in the tournament.

As expected, the next four games were won by a total of 12 points. Each of these four contests literally came down to the last minute of the game before the final outcome was decided. In our regional game against Danville, we were trailing by one point with the ball on our 20 yard line, no time outs and less than two minutes to play. Brian Lauck led an unbelievable 80 yard drive and we kicked a field goal with three seconds to go and won the game 23-21.

In the semi-state game the next week, we traveled to Jasper. They were undefeated and ranked #1. We were leading 10-3 when they scored a touchdown with thirty-two seconds to go in the game. In a gutsy move, they tried for a 2 point conversion — and the win. However, our defense stepped up and stopped them for a 10- 9 victory. For the second year in row — and quite unexpectedly in the eyes of many — we were going to State!

During the long ride home from Jasper, I reflected back on our almost miraculous tournament run. I was now very thankful for Scecina's thoughtful gift, as well as Joe Hollowell's crafty presentation. Since our last four tournament games had come down to the final seconds of each contest, I had no doubt the trophy was a constant reminder of their humiliation. Our players would never again quit or surrender. It would never again be an option. Beyond all else, this was the key factor in us getting back to the State game.

The championship game was against Tipton and, for the first half, our opponent was highly competitive. Nevertheless, our physical style of play began to take its toll on them in the second half. We went on to play perhaps the best that any of the six teams I have coached in a state game has played in the RCA Dome — winning 35-14. I found it ironic that the team had not been expected to be very good after heavy graduation losses — and after being shut out in our season opener. It was this same team who had been embarrassed in their homecoming game and had prompted a lot of people to question their resolve and mental toughness. Moreover, they had fought through the coaching turmoil from the previous year, and had welcomed a new coach from the outside with open arms. Without a doubt, they had come a long way and fought through some difficult obstacles. There was so much gratification derived from this season and this team. I am still moved with pride when I consider what they did.

Finally, our staff had jelled into a cohesive unit ... and we had fun. We worked hard and we enjoyed being around one another. We laughed a lot, and Phil's mischievous personality tended to be at the center of that laughter. This was how I had always hoped our coaching staff would be.

To this day, I still wonder if we would have won the 1994 State Championship without the embarrassing loss to Scecina. I also wonder if it was mere coincidence that Phil Gatts and I just kind of bumped into each other in the summer of 1994. Indeed, God does work in mysterious ways!

CHAPTER 5

Righting the Ship

After back-to-back state championships, the 1995 season held a lot of promise. Jeff Roell and Nick Kidwell, seniors on this team, had each rushed for over 1,100 yards as juniors. We had talented linemen coming back on both sides of the ball, as well as a solid linebacking and defensive secondary core. This senior group also had valuable experience from twelve hard-fought tournament games in the previous two seasons. Last, but not least, most of the returning seniors were both tough and mean. I think we do a good job developing mental and physical toughness during the four years a young man is in our program. However, some kids have a natural mean streak as well. In this context, being mean signifies relishing the opportunity to hit your opponent ... over and over again. If a young man is smart and disciplined in the way he deals with this mentality, he can be a successful football player. Several of the seniors on this team had this trait. It was our job as coaches to corral their aggression and make sure our players were always playing within the guidelines of the game.

As the season began, it seemed all the ingredients were in place for a great season. We had a rare opportunity to become only the second team in Indiana high school history to win three consecutive state football championships. We steamrolled through the first half of our season, playing hard-nosed, physical football. As we approached the end of the regular season, we were on course to finish undefeated heading into tournament play. Interestingly, after starting out so strong, we seemed to be hitting a bit of a plateau as far as our weekly improvement was concerned. Over the years, the vast majority of our teams have shown marked improvement from the first game to the last game of the regular season. Every year, after the last regular season game, we tell our players that the practice season is over and now it is time for the real season (the playoffs) to begin. Strategically, our staff stands by this motto. As competitive people, we want to win every game we play. Yet, we place a high priority on getting our offense, defense, special teams and personnel ready for the playoffs — even if it means sacrificing a little during the regular season. This is all part of the "chess match" I will talk about later in the book.

A big part of our efforts to get ready for the tournament involves getting better each week. During the 1995 season, we were not seeing the degree of improvement we were accustomed to. We were still winning games but, even in victory, I often believed we were winning mostly because we had more talent than the teams we were playing. Some of the games ended with scores closer than they should have been. Something was not quite right, though at the time, I couldn't put my finger on it.

Since two-a-day practices, it was obvious this would not be one of our closer-knit teams. There was a wide range of personalities in our senior class. There were seniors who were great students and others who were not. There was an interesting mix of leadership with this class as well. I have no doubt some of our seniors were as focused and committed to excellence as any we have ever had. Yet, in this class, there was also a faction that worried me when it came to their decisions on weekend and free time activities. We constantly remind the players of the school's strict drug and alcohol policies. In the end, the coaches and players both realize that it boils down to having the right priorities and making the necessary sacrifices to insure the overall team remains as strong as possible. Making the tough decisions requires a great deal of discipline by everyone and is at the core of team chemistry.

During the season, I had trouble figuring out exactly why our team chemistry seemed to be lacking. In spite of the problems, we were winning and finished the regular season undefeated. We went on to be sectional and regional champs — winning twelve games in a row. And, in a repeat of the previous year, we faced Jasper in the semi-state game — this time at Roncalli. Their quarterback, Matt Mauck, would go on to be drafted that next spring to play professional baseball for several seasons in the minor league. After his stint in baseball, he came back to be the starting quarterback for LSU, where he helped lead the school to a national championship. Needless to say, he was a phenomenal athlete and played a vital role in the drubbing they gave us that night.

We had failed in our quest to "three-peat." Even more disappointing than this was the nagging feeling we had as coaches that we weren't able to get this team to play to its potential. Although we finished with a 12-1 record, we still had an empty feeling that extended beyond losing the last game. We knew this group had been capable of so much more.

Towards the end of the school year, some of the seniors came to the coaches before graduation to thank us for all we had done for them during their time at Roncalli. As we sat and talked, I wanted to get their perspective on their senior season — in its entirety. Ultimately, they told me that in the class of twenty senior players, about half of the group had broken the school drug and alcohol policy during the season. Moreover, several had violations on a pretty consistent basis. They even informed me they had heard about a small handful of classmates who had actually violated the policy on the afternoon prior to our semi-state loss. Although they would not give me any names, they made it quite clear that there was a very distinct rift within the team during the season as a result of these infractions. They said there was a great deal of resentment on the part of those who had been disciplined and who had sacrificed to stay loyal and committed to the team and its policies.

After reflecting on what these guys told me, I experienced three distinct emotions:

   ➨ Obviously, I was disappointed in the individuals who had chosen to break team policies. I had always assumed football would be important enough to all of our players that they would never want to do something which would potentially get them suspended from the team or hurt our chances of winning on a Friday night. Quite frankly, I was also disappointed in myself for not recognizing that this had been going on and was the primary factor in the lack of team chemistry.

   ➨ Ironically, I also felt a sense of relief. This was the obvious reason why the team had lacked the cohesiveness of teams from previous years. As odd as it may sound, I was relieved that we were beaten in the tournament. In hindsight, I would have felt terrible if we would have been state champs, regardless of how talented this group was, knowing that such a significant number of our seniors broke policy and failed to honor their commitment.

   ➨ Most of all, I felt heartbroken for those who had been committed to doing the right thing and what was best for the team. I have no doubt this senior class had some of the hardest working and most devoted players I have ever coached. They deserved better than they got. At the same time, I felt the pang of regret for the young men who weren't committed to the team and who had other things that were more important to them at that time. I know as they get older, they will have to live with that regret for the rest of their lives.

The primary reason I have gone into so much detail on this topic is because this situation was another turning point in my career as a coach. This was an obvious example of the dissension and resentment that can be caused by a lack of commitment among teams. In the '93, '94 and '95 seasons, we had a combined record of 38 wins, 3 losses, and two State Championships. Yet, we had also had a season where our coaching staff was torn apart and another in which the players were divided by strife. It became painfully apparent to me that there was a profound difference between having a few good seasons and building a great program.

I once heard a wise coach say that you must have three things in place before you can build a great program. You must first have a solid administration that understands and appreciates the value of athletics in the school system. You must next piece together a coaching staff that is willing to work hard, stay loyal to you and the other assistants, and be committed to being good role models for kids. Finally, you must get your players to do the right thing, to the best of their ability, all of the time! I felt like we have always had a great administration at Roncalli, and that we had now assembled a coaching staff that met all of these specifications. However, we obviously still had work to do with our players.

Prior to the 1996 season, with our focus on building a PROGRAM, I was wise enough to understand that the team goes as the seniors go. The '96 seniors were pretty average as far as size and sheer athletic ability, but they were very intelligent and knew they did not want to go through what the class before them had experienced. They understood their degree of success would directly correlate to their ability to pull their class into a tight-knit group.

As I met with the seniors at the start of the summer, I wanted to re-emphasize to them the importance of team loyalty and the unity that is created when everyone is committed to doing the right thing for the welfare of the team. Interestingly enough, this group was light years ahead of me. They had already begun to draft a player contract they asked me to read. The contract basically stated that it was a privilege, not a right, to play Roncalli football. Since so many good men had sacrificed so much before them to create the Roncalli tradition, it was their duty to do everything in their power to carry on the legacy. By signing the contract, every player was vowing not to break the school's drug and alcohol policy. If any player then chose to break the contract, he would promise to turn his equipment in and quit the team.

This document was the beginning of a solution! The real beauty of it was that they came up with it on their own and wanted it to be mandatory for all players to sign before they could play. I was excited for this team; this was a bold move and I knew we were taking a huge step forward towards building a program. I still remain grateful to this senior class for their heart and dedication.

Aaron Irwin was a big All-State tackle on this team, but was about the only senior in the class with much size. In spite of this, we lost only one game in the regular season, and went on to finish with a 10-2 season record. Our second loss was in the sectionals, a 14-7 heartbreaker to the eventual state champs. Unlike the previous season, we saw noticeable improvement as the season progressed, and our coaches felt like we were getting the most out of our players. Overall, it proved to be a wonderful season.

Heading into the 1997 season, we were reclassified up into 4A football. We had always been one of the larger 3A teams in the state. On the other hand, for the '97 and '98 seasons, we were the smallest 4A school in the tournament. Our '97 team was an outstanding group and very fun to watch. Adam Stephenson and Drew McGlinchey were perhaps the two best quarterbacks we have ever had in the same class, and Adam went on to pass for well over 1,000 yards as we used his talents to run multiple formations and spread out our offense more than usual.

Our starting tailback, Sean Schembra, was a gifted athlete and an unbelievable football player. Sean ran the 40-yard dash in 4.4 seconds, and could bench press 350 lbs. He also had great hands and an incredible work ethic. He never lost a wind sprint at the end of practice. With his humble demeanor, he was a great role model for the kids in the Roncalli community. He went on to have a great career at Ball State University. Today, he is a fireman, and helps coach our wide receivers and defensive backs. Both of my own sons continue to look up to him as a positive role model.

By the time Sean graduated, he had set sixteen school rushing and scoring records. He had led our offense to a very exciting season. In our first year in 4A football, however, we lost in the sectional final and finished with a 10-2 season. Like the previous year, this team lived by the contract and gave us everything they had. Our two victories over Cathedral during this season were among the most exciting I had coached at Roncalli, and were vital steps towards establishing the great "program" we were seeking.

The senior class of the following '98 season was an interesting mix of characters. This group was very bright, and might have had the highest overall GPA of any group of seniors we have ever had. They were also very close-knit and fun-loving. I immediately nicknamed them the Wolfpack, because they did everything together. The senior girls in their class were envious and somewhat resentful of their commitment to football and to each other. As the head football coach, this was beautiful!

This class had more than its share of personality. Eddie Keller, who had carried the nickname "Crunchy" since he was in grade school, was a big All-State tackle and standout heavyweight wrestler. He also had a great sense of humor and an amazing singing voice. It was a weekly ritual for the seniors to go out to dinner at a local smorgasbord the night before a game — and for Eddie to break into song afterwards. He always had a voracious appetite and it seemed that for him to serenade everyone in the restaurant was his way of showing approval for a delicious meal. Although he had a wide variety of songs he could perform, without question, the most requested was "If I Were King of the Forest" from the Wizard of Oz. Eddie had played the cowardly lion in his eighth grade school musical, and it was always amusing to hear this 300-lb. mountain of a man with a beautiful, opera-like voice perform this song.

Eddie is now a Social Studies teacher at Roncalli and our varsity line coach. Even now, his performance is requested often when our staff and significant others go out to dinner.

Another one of the ringleaders in the '98 senior cast of characters was Matt Hollowell, our President's second oldest son. Matt is very bright, witty and can make almost anyone laugh. During the fall of his senior year, most of the Wolfpack was sitting in the back corner of the cafeteria during lunch. I always set up a TV and VCR where our players can sit together during lunch and watch video footage of our upcoming opponent. During this lunch period, there was a particularly vigilant teacher carrying out her duties as cafeteria monitor. Watching from the faculty table across the cafeteria, I could tell the Wolfpack was probably in the midst of another of their good-natured pranks. I could see Matt sitting in the middle of the group, kind of crouched over as if he were trying to hide something. As I looked closer, it appeared he was talking on a cell phone. Since cell phones are not allowed in school, and especially since the heads-up monitor was close by, it was only a matter of seconds before she swooped in for the kill. Matt, startled that he had been discovered, tried to hide the phone.

"Hand it over, Matt," the monitor stated flatly. After a three- or four-second pause, Matt replied, "Well ... okay." He then proceeded to hand her the remote control for the VCR, which he had been pretending to talk into. The whole group began to giggle — and, fortunately, so did the monitor. She knew she had been caught — hook, line and sinker.

A few weeks later at practice, when we were working on special teams, Pat Schaub, our starting tailback and a senior co-captain approached me saying "Coach, we need to talk." Pat was also very bright and was extremely intense — both on the practice and game field. In fact, he went on to rush for over 2,000 yards that season.

Since his demeanor was usually very serious on the field, I was immediately concerned that he would seek me out in the middle of practice with the need to talk. "What is it, Pat?" I asked with obvious concern in my voice. "Well, Coach … I found out somebody on the team is in violation of our drug and alcohol contract and I felt it was my duty to turn them in." Instantly, I felt a sick feeling in my stomach and knew I was going to have to kick someone off the team. "Well, Pat. Who is it?" I asked. "Coach, he's standing right over there!" With this, he pointed over towards Matt Hollowell, who was one of Pat's best friends.

Matt was standing by himself, helmet hanging in his hand. As I looked closer, I could see that Matt had a nasty, old cigarette butt he had picked up off the ground hanging out of his mouth, and had a tough guy snarl on his upper lip. As he watched practice for a few seconds, he pretended to take one last puff on the cigarette before he flicked it away with his free hand — again, in the tough guy fashion. As I heard some of the nearby Wolfpack begin to snicker, I knew that like the unsuspecting lunch monitor, I too had been caught.

I have always appreciated the wittiness of the '98 seniors and their wonderful sense of humor. What I admired most, however, was their tremendous sense of unity and family. They were undoubtedly one of the best football teams I have ever coached. They finished the regular season undefeated, and our defense led the state of Indiana in the category of fewest points allowed. Scott Stewart, one of our assistant coaches, had taken over the defensive coordinator's position for this season. Phil had to take a one-year sabbatical from coaching when his high school aged daughter had to undergo major surgery. Scott filled in and did a remarkable job. In spite of their love of laughter, when it came time to play, this team was as focused and intense as any group we have ever had. Their tremendous work ethic also made them as deserving to win as any team we have ever had.

Unfortunately, we lost to Avon High School that year — our second season in 4A football — on a last second field goal. Even now, I haven't quite figured this out. In the second half, we led but in 17 of the last 22 plays, we made key mistakes that proved to be costly. Dropped passes and kicks, penalties, players lining up incorrectly and missed assignments all combined to cause our defeat. Up to this point, the team had done everything right and deserved to win. To this day, this is still one of the hardest losses I have ever had to deal with. I felt like this team had done everything right to deserve a State Championship. Patrick Shaub was named Indianapolis Player of the Year. Steve Eckhart and Chris Price were 4.0 students and two of the best linebackers our school has ever had. John Harrington, the team's quarterback and starting corner, is now a full time coach, along with Patrick Schaub, on our freshman staff.

As I reflect back on the '96, '97 and '98 seasons, we won ten games each year, but did not win a state championship. However, we made huge strides towards improving the program. One that has the ability to change young lives in a positive way; a program that can help young men along the sometimes troubled road to manhood.

Role Model
An Athlete's Responsibility

*To the world you may mean very little,
but to someone little you may mean the world.*

CHAPTER 6

The Family Man

The love of a family — I don't think there's another factor in our lives that evokes as much passion or emotion. Along with our faith in God, our families play a vital role in who we are, where we have been and where we are going. I have mentioned some of the people who have influenced my life, through athletics, in a very powerful way. I have also discussed my growth as a person through my early seasons as a coach. My family, as well, has had a profound impact on my career and personal development.

God has truly blessed me with a large and wonderful family. More than any other factor in my life, my family has shaped who I am, my morals and faith in God and ultimately, how I have chosen to conduct myself as an adult.

I briefly mentioned my parents in Chapter One. What I did not include is that I respect and cherish my mom and dad as much as any two people on the face of the earth. Mom is eighty-three and Dad is eighty-one, and I feel absolutely blessed to still have them both as a vital part of my life and the lives of my children. Raising a family of eight children was certainly a challenge for them. Although we were raised without much wealth or material possessions, there was never any doubt that our parents loved us very much.

My mother is one of the most unselfish people I have ever known. She has sacrificed and given everything she has to try to make sure her children have what they need. She is also one of the strongest people I know. Over the years, she has fought through a near-fatal car accident, joint replacement, severe arthritis and breast cancer. Through it all, I have rarely heard her complain, since she would never want to burden her children with her problems. As we were growing up, she was our primary teacher in matters relating to God and the church. Every Sunday, she would make sure all eight of us were fed, dressed and loaded up to head to Sunday school and the weekly church service. It was through this determined introduction to God, and through watching my mother do her best to raise eight children, that I began to understand the attributes of unconditional love. Even at eighty-three years of age, she still ranks right there with my wife and two daughters as one of the four most beautiful women I have ever known.

Each year, on February 14th, I drop off a card — sometimes in her mailbox or perhaps on her front door. It's usually a silly, homemade card asking her to be my Valentine. Knowing her, she wouldn't want anything too plush or expensive. Yet, I want her to know how much I love her, that she is still beautiful to me and that she will forever hold a special place in my heart. She deserves that!

Likewise, my father was a very hard worker and a great role model. His father died when he was thirteen years old — in the middle of the Great Depression. As a result, he lived a rather hard childhood and wasn't able to finish high school. For a time, he even had to leave his family to live in the Masonic Home in Franklin, Indiana. As a young man, he became a welder and continued that career until his retirement. Being a caring father and provider, he tried to work as much overtime as possible. Throughout my childhood, most days, I recall him coming home late, dirty and exhausted.

A healthy combination of respect and fear made me careful to stay on Dad's good side. In fact, to this day, I can't remember ever "smarting off" to him — it was simply unthinkable.

Although he was not much of a church-goer, I have always considered him to be a spiritual man. He has always read the Bible and lived his life accordingly. Never one for crowds, my father would much rather be sitting along the river somewhere, fishing pole in hand, visiting Mother Nature.

While I was growing up, my dad wasn't overly expressive with words of love, yet we all knew he loved us deeply. Some of my best childhood memories are of Dad frying up a big batch of hamburgers and fries on a Friday night. If we were lucky, we might even get a bottle of pop to top off the meal. As he has gotten older, it has become much easier for Dad to express his love for his children and grandchildren. Every time I see him, we hug and tell each other "I love you." I think he needs and appreciates this as much as I do.

Dad has taught me many things over the years: to work hard, be humble, be thankful for what you have and, above all else, to love God. The most valuable and cherished lesson, however, has come from witnessing my parents' sixty-one years of marriage. During that span, there have certainly been troubled times, but they have always stuck to the vows they made before God so many years ago. I have heard the best way for a father to show his children he loves them is to show his children that he loves their mother. For close to a year, my mother has struggled to get around and has relied on using a walker. Watching my father be so devoted to her has made me prouder than ever to be his son. I can't image a better example of what it means to be a man. Now more than ever, I hope that someday I can grow up to be like him.

As I said before, my parents were great role models and although as a youngster, I used to wish we had more money, nicer clothes, etc. I now understand that you don't need wealth or material possessions to have integrity and class. I have also grown to understand that what matters most is how you use the gifts God has given you. I am forever grateful to my parents for teaching me this lesson.

Earlier in the book, I mentioned my older brothers, Sam and Kim. Next in line were my two older sisters, Roxie and Marguerite, who are three and four years my senior respectively. I also have three younger sisters, Becky, Bonita and Jenny, who are all one year behind the other. In all, there are eight of us and we were born over the course of eleven years.

The days when Mom and Dad both worked were quite challenging — especially during summer vacations. Imagine eight siblings, age five through sixteen, at home for the entire summer. When our parents (who were "co-Commanders in Chief") were gone, Sam was left in charge as our "General" since he was the oldest. Kim, as second oldest, was the "Sergeant at Arms" and, each day, they were responsible for making sure that the household chores were done. The younger six, of course, were the foot soldiers and the primary workers. If our work wasn't done to the General's satisfaction, sit ups, push ups and laps around the house were in order. Given that Sam was also the proud owner of a Daisy BB gun, the possibility of being a victim of the firing squad insured that we would all remain subservient.

For the sake of entertainment, the General and his Sergeant at Arms would periodically make a big batch of popcorn. The foot soldiers would then participate in hand-to-hand combat drills — gladiator style. The winner of each brawl would get to take the seat of honor next to the General, grab a few handfuls of popcorn for sustenance and receive the rest of the day off from work detail. For the losers, however, there would be more laps around the house and additional work. By the time I was about eight, I could whip my older sisters pretty consistently. As a result, my brothers began to bring in recruits from around the neighborhood. Ironically, these battles would pay off in later years when we laced up the gloves in my buddy's garage.

Since Sam and Kim had us convinced they would torture us if Mom and Dad ever caught wind of their war games, my sisters and I never squealed on them. One afternoon, after Sam had watched an old western on TV, he grabbed his BB gun and ordered me out on the street in front of the house. His words, "Now, I want you to dance!" had me slightly alarmed — especially since I didn't have any shoes on. In short order, he had me high stepping as he yelled, "Yee-haw!!" and fired several rounds of BB's at my feet. Suddenly, I yelped as I felt a sharp, gripping pain in the big toe of my right foot. Sam immediately grabbed me and reminded me of the consequences if I told Mom or Dad. I could see a hole in my toe, but the worst part of the pain subsided quickly so I assumed the BB had just bounced off. My toe remained sore for several weeks, but I didn't dare tell my parents. The consequences would have been far more painful! About three months later, I was taking a shower when I felt another sharp pain in my big toe. I looked down just in time to see a BB pop out and roll down the drain.

Sam, Kim and I shared a bedroom. In it, Sam had a single bed, and Kim and I had bunk beds. Of course, Kim claimed the bottom bunk and advised me to stay out of his bed. One day, when I thought he would be gone for the entire day, I snuggled into his bunk for a quick nap. He came back sooner than expected and I was suddenly awakened by his sing-song proclamation, "Bruuuuce, wake uuuuup. I have something for you!" To my great horror, I looked across the room to find him standing there with three darts in his hand. After reminding me that he had warned me to stay out of his bed, he said, "Now, just lay real still and you should be okay!" Then, he proceeded to throw the first dart and, since I was laying on my back, I watched it streak across the room and zip into the wall — about twelve inches over my chest. His next warning, "Don't move and don't make a sound, or I'll drill ya' with the next one!" was not terribly reassuring. I watched in a mild state of terror as the next dart stuck soundly into the mattress — about six inches below my right side. Of course, I could tell what he was doing. He was trying to get closer with each throw and, frankly, I didn't like the prospect of his little game. Be that as it may, he still had one more dart in his arsenal so the best I could do was lay very still and pray for accuracy. I'm not sure where he was aiming, but the next thing I knew, the third dart was lodged in the right side of my chest. I had an interesting reaction — I opened my mouth to scream but nothing came out. Kim flew across the room in one swift movement and covered my mouth with one had and removed the dart with the other. I was then presented with the usual threats of death and torture if I told Mom or Dad, followed by an order to get into my own bed (I think he didn't want me leaving any blood or evidence on his bedspread.)

Today, three of my siblings have moved to other states — Sam lives in Florida, Kim is in Virginia and Jenny, the youngest, is in Georgia — and I miss each of them very much. My other four sisters still live in Indiana and I try to see them as much as possible. Every year, usually in July, all eight kids come back to Indy for a week to take part in the "Scifres Reunion." It's great to be able to reminisce with stories about our childhood and we laugh a lot in the process too. As the years pass, I feel blessed to consider them all to be among my best friends. As I stated before, our large family is a blessing and while the physical scars continue to fade with age, our relationships have proven indestructible and full of life and love.

After Jackie and I were married, we started a family of our own. Our oldest, Luke, is fourteen, Abby is twelve, Caleb is ten and Meggie is eight. So we go boy, girl, boy, girl and they are all almost exactly two years apart. As a matter of fact, all four birthdays are in June and July. If you do the math, all four of them had to be conceived sometime in the fall — during football season. Ironically, my wife doesn't even like me during football season since I am so preoccupied and am seldom home. Go figure! Regardless, God blessed us with four beautiful children. I can remember my mom telling me, many years before I was even married, that I could never understand the fullest extent of love until I had children of my own. I now know exactly what she was talking about. I realize that each of our four kids are very precious gifts from God, handpicked especially for Jackie and me.

Luke was born during the summer right after my first year at Roncalli. As a result, he has been around Roncalli football ever since he was a baby. His dream is to play for the Rebels, followed by four years of college football. Then, he wants to come back and coach at Roncalli. When he was about three years old, we were sitting in our backyard with Jackie's mom. Luke had gone inside and came back out with my whistle around his neck, my coaching hat pulled way down over his ears and my clipboard under his arm. He jogged over to his grandma and said, "Hi, I'm the coach." We all had a good laugh, mostly because his mannerisms were so much like mine. Over the years, Jackie has continued to remark on how much Luke reminds her of me.

Luke has always been very bright with a great sense of humor. When he was around four years old, he and Jackie were wrestling around on the family room floor. He told Jackie to wait just a minute and he ran upstairs. When he returned, all he was wearing were some of my long insulated socks pulled all the way up to the top of his thighs. He got down in a great wrestler's stance and said, "Come on, Mom. Let's wrestle!" Fighting back laughter, Jackie said, "You know, Luke, you're becoming a big boy now so you really should go back upstairs and get some clothes on." Luke innocently asked, "Why, Mom?" and I was impressed with her quick and clever comeback as she said, "Well, as you get older, your little wiener might freeze and fall off." Without missing a beat, Luke came back with, "Wow, Mom. Is that what happened to you?" From that point on, Jackie and I decided we would both be a little more factual when it came time to discuss human anatomy.

Luke is now entering his teen years and is both tall and fast with the potential to become a pretty good athlete. He is an affectionate young man, and he and I have an extremely close relationship. He recently told Jackie I am his best friend. I firmly believe this is the highest compliment I could ever receive from my fourteen-year-old son. He has always seemed to really enjoy spending time with his dad. I often pray that God will help me to always be a strong and loving father and a constant Christian role model in my children's lives. In doing so, I hope Luke will always know how much I love him and how very proud I am to be his father. As he draws closer to becoming a Rebel, and having me for a coach, I pray regularly that God will grant me the wisdom to coach him in a fair and positive way. I truly don't want to be overly critical of him or treat him differently than I would any other player. While coaching your own flesh and blood may have its advantages (and some drawbacks) I have to trust that the Lord will guide me appropriately when dealing with them.

Our second son, Caleb, usually goes by the nickname Cal. Our players usually call him "Big Cal" because he is very tall and big for his age. Luke has always played quarterback or running back, but Cal is definitely the lineman type. His hand-eye skills and overall coordination haven't yet caught up with his size and it seems he's always running into things with reckless abandon. As I said, he has lineman written all over him. He's really like a big Teddy Bear, and is irresistibly huggable. One of life's greatest pleasures is listening to him laugh and giggle when something tickles his fancy.

One of my favorite Cal stories is from when he was about five years old. It was around Christmas and the rest of the family had gone to bed. Once I had turned out all of the lights except for the Christmas tree, Cal snuggled up on my lap. After he had been still for several minutes, I assumed he had fallen asleep. Staring at the lights, I had one of those delicious moments in time when I wanted to freeze everything for a long time so I could just sit there and hold my son. Suddenly, Cal's head popped up, he looked at the tree for several seconds and asked me a question that I'm sure had been eating away at him for several minutes. "Daddy, do you think Santa Claus could beat up Jesus?" he asked. Knowing this had probably been bothering him for a good long while, I knew this was one of those rare opportunities a father seldom has to say something profound that could change his son's life forever. So, I thoughtfully replied, "Aw, naw, Cal. It wouldn't even be close!" He was so astounded with my infinite wisdom that he immediately put his head back on my chest and was sawing logs within sixty seconds.

This episode confirmed two things in my mind. First, Cal must have really wanted me to tell him that Santa Claus wouldn't stand a chance against Jesus. Faith formation in our children is one of the primary tasks God gives to us as parents. It's important that we don't fumble the ball in this area! Secondly, I felt confirmation of how lucky and blessed I am to have two sons to call my own. I pray that God will always help me to be a loving father to them both and someone whom they can look up to and be proud of.

When my sons were born, I knew I would love them always with all my heart. I had always dreamed of having sons of my own, and they are both perfect gifts from God. They have been an endless source of love, pride and joy.

As a parent, I have also learned that God reserves a very special place in a father's heart that only his daughters can fill. Abby, our oldest daughter, is a natural at just about everything she does. Whether it's her grades, sports, art, dancing or writing, everything just seems to come to her easily. Like Luke, she's tall, fast and athletic. Of course, I may be biased, but she is also beautiful like her mom. Abby also has a wonderful sense of humor and can be quite the cut-up when she's at home. However, around others, she can be very shy and self-conscious. Her sister is very different in this regard.

As the youngest, Meggie loves an audience. She might even have a career ahead of her as a standup comedienne. There's seldom a day that goes by in which I don't get a big laugh out of something she says or does. Her facial expressions and exaggerated gestures amuse us all. Her tendency to wear silly outfits around the house keeps things interesting. She is very affection-ate and gives some of the world's best hugs, though she some-times struggles to give her dad as many as he says he needs. When we found out that Jackie was pregnant with Meggie — our fourth child — we were immediately concerned with how we could survive financially with another mouth to feed. As al-ways, God knew what he was doing. It's hard to put into words how deeply our children have blessed our lives.

When I was younger, I used to vow that I would never allow a female to wrap me around her little finger. I just never felt it would be in my best interest. Yet, Jackie says I am oblivi-ous to the spell my daughters have cast upon me. Nevertheless, I know they have both touched my life in a way that only daugh-ters can. Moreover, I know my life will never be the same be-cause of it.

Of course, as the father of two beautiful girls, I'm dreading the day when they're old enough to date. However, I am confi-dent that word will get around quickly that Coach Scifres has some very high standards regarding how his daughters are to be treated by potential suitors. Even now, I can envision myself standing in the doorway to greet the young man as he arrives. I will be waiting with a very strong ally in each hand. My good friend Louis will be to my right. Now, mind you, this is just a nickname. His real first name is Louisville and his last name is Slugger. If the young man who walks up is into hip-hop fash-ion, and is sporting the "sag" look, or gives me any indication that he isn't sure how to keep his pants pulled up properly, the ally in my left hand will immediately be put to use. It's called a staple gun. Needless to say, I intend to be a very "hands on" parent when it comes time for my children to date.

Naturally, my wife Jackie is the glue that holds our family together. In the eighteen years we have been married, she has had more of a positive impact on my life than any other adult. I have often said she and I have a "Beauty and the Beast" rela-tionship. It doesn't take much imagination to figure out that

BEYOND THE GOAL LINE

she's the beauty and I'm the beast! At 5' 6" and 115 lbs., she certainly doesn't look like a woman with four children who is approaching her mid-forties. Without a doubt, she has aged more gracefully than I. She is one of the most beautiful women I have ever met, but it is her inner beauty that continues to capture my heart. In many respects, our young lives were very similar since she grew up in a family with seven children and relatively humble means. We have often discussed that it's a good thing neither of us came from a lot of money because it has allowed us to keep things in proper perspective and truly appreciate what we have.

Her father passed away when she was sixteen and her mother, Laura, did an amazing job raising the family on her own. Jackie's mom is genuinely a wonderful woman with a great deal of inner strength. I've heard many times that you can tell a lot about the type of woman a young lady will become by looking at her mother. With this in mind, I knew I made a great choice in marrying Jackie. I have nothing but love and respect for her mother, Laura Reinhart.

Among the seven siblings is Jackie's identical twin, Jennifer. Over the years, I have teased that I got the better looking of the two but, even today, family members still can't tell them apart. As a testament to the bonds of our close family, Jennifer and her husband, Brian Avery, live quite close to us — across the street and about three houses down. They have three children about the same ages as ours and they are all inseparable. As fate would have it, Brian is the Athletic Director at Franklin Central, our neighborhood rival. It has been a wonderful blessing to have Jennifer and Brian so close. She's a wonderful aunt and loves our children like her own.

I also have a great deal of love and affection for the rest of Jackie's family. She has another sister who is one year older, and four brothers — all of whom still live in Seymour. Whenever we visit, we are guaranteed a good time because her family, like mine, is very close knit. Since my own brothers live out of state, her brothers have taken me under their wings as part of the family. I am grateful for having been adopted into another large and wonderful family.

People have often made the observation that Jackie and I have a very close and unique relationship. After being married about a year, she and I went on a hayride in Seymour with about twenty other couples. The hosts had all of us play a game in which each couple filled out a sheet with around twenty questions about your spouse — including their favorite movie, color, shoe size, etc. The answers were compared and the couple with the most correct answers were declared the winners. Even though most of the other couples had been married longer than us, Jackie and I won easily. I have always felt that she and I communicate very well with each other, and I believe this is at the core of any good relationship. I know we have a special marriage because after eighteen years of marriage not only do I still love my wife very much, I am also still very much in love with her.

There are three factors that help me know this is true, and I'll rank them from least to greatest:

🐚 I still feel a very strong physical attraction to her. She is truly more beautiful to me today than the day we met. Often times, I have difficulty sleeping at night — particularly in the fall. Frequently, I will just lay there and watch her sleep, and wonder what someone as beautiful as she could see in someone like me. Sometimes during the day, she will catch me looking at her and will ask if something is wrong. There's just something incredibly attractive about her — knowing that she is the woman who has faithfully loved me for so many years. To me, she is most beautiful when she is surrounded by our children. She is such a wonderful mother and all four of our kids just adore her. Watching her play and cuddle and interact with our children makes me fall in love all over again.

🐚 She still makes me happy. After all these years, when we meet somewhere, she still lights up the room when she walks in, and brings an immediate smile to my face. Although she comes across as somewhat shy, she is very witty and can really make me laugh. I continue to enjoy spending time with her, even when it's just the two of us chatting quietly.

☙ Being with her has made me a better person. I have no doubt that my Christian faith is stronger because of her. I began going to church with her soon after we met. She and I both felt that we should raise our children in a strong Christian household. Throughout our marriage, she has also been a good sounding board for me — both personally and professionally — particularly when my inclination may be to do or say something brash. However, first and foremost, she is simply a good person and I am very proud to be her husband. God gave me a wonderful gift when He sent her into my life.

Our football team recently received our 2004 State Championship ring. It commemorates our third consecutive 4A State Championship and, since it is custom made, it is really a beautiful ring. When it arrived Luke was admiring it and asked, "Dad, which of the rings you've won means the most to you?" Now, I have to say that as a coach I've been very blessed. We've won six State Championships in the past twelve years. I also have a State Runner Up ring from my last year as head track coach at Lawrence Central. In addition, I have two other rings that the ring company gave me for being repeat champs. All together, I have nine rings from which to choose and thought this was the perfect opportunity to make a point to my children. For the first time ever, I put all nine rings on different fingers.

Then, I told them, "Now. I'm going to take these off — one by one — until I get to the one that means the most to me. The one that most represents hard work, loyalty, sacrifice and accomplishment." After that, I began to take each of them off and put them back in their boxes — pausing long enough so they could see some of the years and to pique their curiosity. When there was one State ring left on my hand, I quickly covered it with my other hand, took it off and put it in the box before anyone could see what year it was.

Luke protested, "Dad, we didn't get to see which one means the most to you!" To this I replied, "Yes you did because I still have it on." At this point, I raised my left hand, where my wedding band was on my ring finger. "This is the ring that means the most to me. It represents years of hard work, loyalty, sacrifice and accomplishment. It is, by far, the ring I am most proud of and the one I never take off!"

I'm not sure this was the answer they were looking for. Regardless, I wanted them to know that there is nothing in my life that I am prouder of than the fact that I am married to their mother. I believe there is no better way for me to show my love for them.

Ironically, as a child I used to wonder what it would be like to be from a smaller family so we might be able to afford more clothes, a bigger house or a nicer car. As an adult, I now understand that true happiness comes from the love of a family, not from material possessions. I am forever grateful to my parents for teaching me this valuable lesson. It is now my responsibility to pass these lessons on to my children. This is one of the true blessings of being a family man.

Success in this life is not measured by what you own,
but rather how much you are loved by your own.

CHAPTER 7

The Covenant

"Most men lead lives of quiet desperation." Henry David Thoreau wrote these words 150 years ago as he reflected on the void that exists in most of our hearts during our time on Earth. By the late 1990's, I was approaching the end of my first decade as head coach. I felt that, in most regards, I had my life and career heading in the right direction. Jackie and I were happily married with four beautiful children, I was teaching and coaching at a first-rate school, and I was surrounded each day by some incredible people. My colleagues at work as well as the young people I taught and coached were not only outstanding but fun to be around as well. We had developed a close and loyal coaching staff and we worked hard to take steps forward in building a sound program — one that would teach our players more than just X's and O's. It seemed like everything in my life was finally in place.

Yet, being in my early forties, I was at a point in my life where I began to reflect more on my own personal and spiritual growth. Like a lot of people who are entering "mid life," I was beginning to realize that I wanted more ... and it had nothing to do with money, possessions or state championships.

In the last chapter, I mentioned that my mother played a pivotal role in the development of my faith as a child. I was raised in a Protestant home and my family attended Camby Community Church, a small, interdenominational congregation about five miles from our home. As part of this church, I grew up believing in tolerance among all faiths. I still believe today that we are all praying to the same God, and as long as we make an effort to live our lives according to the example set by Jesus Christ, we are all making strides toward becoming the person God wants us to be. I also believe we should be tolerant and respectful of the traditions inherent with other denominations.

A few years ago, someone asked me why I choose to believe in God. I have always considered myself to be a pretty logical person (although I'm sure there are some who have witnessed my play calling on Friday nights who might question this!) A simple, yet logical and somewhat philosophical way of explaining why I choose to believe in God can be broken down into three parts:

☞ If I live my life on Earth as if there is no such thing as God or Heaven, and then at the hour of my death realize they do exist, what will eternity have in store for me?

☞ If I live my life as if God and Heaven do exist, and find out at the hour of my death that there is no such thing, at least I will have lived a good life and will have helped to make the world around me a better place.

☞ If I believe in God and Heaven, choose to live my life accordingly and ultimately find out they do exist, I will have lived my life on this Earth with a purpose and will be rewarded with eternal peace and happiness. What better reason could there be to believe?

Furthermore, as a Christian, I believe in the life, death and resurrection of Jesus Christ. There have been many books written about the historical accuracy of these Biblical accounts and without delving into all of this, I believe simply that Jesus was sent to teach us how to live our lives, how to treat other people and, above all else, how to love and serve God. During our time on Earth, I believe it is our duty to try to live according to the example set by Jesus Christ. I also believe in the ultimate reward of Heaven.

The same person who asked why I choose to believe in God also asked how I can believe in something I can't experience through the five senses. I answered that I see and hear God all the time through the people who have touched my life and the lives of others by doing Godly things. Another example is that while you can't see the wind, you can observe its results and you can certainly feel it as well. Likewise, I see the results of God's love in my life on a daily basis and, like the wind, I can actually feel Him touching me. Often times, especially when I am alone and quiet, I try to pray so I can give God my undivided attention. It is during these quiet moments of prayer that I feel His presence — usually in the form of a warm, tingling sensation throughout my body.

Again, like the wind, I can't see Him but I can certainly feel Him and I know He is there. This experience, and the resulting inner peace and calm, are better than any drug that money can buy. In my heart this affirms, beyond any shadow of a doubt, that there is a God and that He must love me very much.

My wife is from a large, devout Catholic family. Even though I was raised Protestant, I was teaching at Roncalli when we met. Since I was becoming more familiar with the Catholic faith, it was easy for me to attend church with her on Sundays. Jackie knew me well enough to know that it wouldn't have been a good idea to demand that I convert to Catholicism. In fact, it would have been a sure fire way to guarantee that I wouldn't do it! However, she and I were both in agreement that we would raise our children in the Catholic church and they would attend Catholic schools. We remain faithful, as our parents were, to making certain our family attends mass and because of this, I had often times considered becoming Catholic. One of the deterring factors to converting was that the RCIA classes began in the fall — usually around Labor Day weekend — and extended until the following Easter. The fall months are so hectic and stressful that going through the program always seemed out of the question; and yet my logic here always seemed meager.

One day, in the Spring of 1999, Joe Hollowell and I were talking about the RCIA program. He suddenly volunteered, "If you ever decide to become Catholic, I would be happy to be your sponsor." His offer caught my attention because I had always used my shortage of time as a weak excuse not to do it. Yet, here was a man with eleven children who was extending an offer to devote some of his time to assist me in converting to the Catholic faith. My "lack of time" excuse no longer seemed valid. I thanked him for the offer and told him I would need some time to think and pray about it.

Before I could convert, there was something else to which I wanted to be committed. By the spring of 1999, I had already received a couple of offers to take higher paying jobs as the head coach at larger public schools. I must admit, it was tempting. At the time, one of the jobs would have included a $20,000 per year pay increase. The other was not far from that. When you multiply that number times twenty to twenty-five years left in a career, we're looking at close to half a million dollars of potential income.

Not only could that pay for college educations for my children, there were other benefits as well; retirement funds, better health insurance, etc. Certainly, it could help alleviate a number of financial concerns for my family. Yet, I found it unbearable to even remotely consider standing in front of our team to tell them I would be leaving because I needed to make more money. I would always get a lump in my throat, my eyes would well up with tears and I would invariably get a sick feeling in my stomach. I knew this would be one of the hardest things I would ever have to do. The more I prayed about it, the more convinced I became that God really wanted me to stay at Roncalli. Likewise, as I prayed about converting to Catholicism, I came to believe this was what God wanted for me as well.

Around this same time, I was listening to a radio interview

with Tony Dungy, who was then the coach of the Tampa Bay Bucaneers. I have always admired him for the positive Christian role model he has been as a professional sports figure. Something he said has stayed with me, "Commit everything you do in life to the Lord and you will be successful." He went on to say that this holds true in all aspects of your life. As I prayed and reflected on his statement, I became convinced that in fact God did want me to commit myself to doing his work at Roncalli and joining the rest of my family as a member of the Catholic Church was part of the "covenant." I felt very good about my decision.

With Joe Hollowell as my sponsor, I entered the RCIA program in the fall of 1999. Although it was somewhat time consuming, especially during the season, it was enjoyable and ended up being a great learning experience for me. Along with learning a lot about the history and traditions of the Catholic faith, I felt I was recommitting my life to God's work. I felt as though my vision for my life was clearer than ever before. I was very excited about the opportunity to receive the Eucharist, the body and blood of Christ, for the first time. A few weeks before Easter, Rosalie Hawthorne, our RCIA director, informed us that we could begin making the sign of the cross during mass if we would like. However, I decided to wait until Easter, when my Catholicity would be "official." The day I was welcomed into the church, making the sign of the cross for the first time was a very powerful experience for me. My whole body was consumed by the warm, tingling sensation of God's presence. Even today, the sign of the cross is moving for me. It serves as a constant reminder of the thorns thrust into Christ's head, and the spikes driven into his feet and hands. This is a concept I hope I never take for granted.

Today, I feel like I am a better Christian, not because I have become Catholic, but because my faith means a great deal more now than it ever did. As a result of my upbringing in an interdenominational church, I think I have a deep respect for all denominations and I don't think I am better than anyone else because of my chosen faith — I simply don't think God wants us to feel that way. At this point in my life, I feel very comfortable with where I am in my relationship with God. Yet I also know that just like any kind of friendship or relationship, it is an ongoing process and will continue to require work and effort on my part. I am looking forward to making this relationship grow stronger.

We try to incorporate God in as much of our daily routine as possible. Each day at the end of practice, we bring everyone into a tight circle where we all take a knee and grab a teammate's hand. Players volunteer to lead us in a closing prayer. It's usually our seniors, but occasionally an underclassman will take the lead. We also pray as a team before and after games.

The final phase of my covenant with God has to do with me applying my renewed faith. I have made the commitment that I want to make it to Heaven and that, ultimately, I want to take as many people with me as I can. Other than my own children, I think the group I have the most positive influence over are the young men I coach on a daily basis. This influence carries over through our whole staff and our responsibility to be good role models. One of our first rules is that no one in our program is allowed to swear. If a player accidentally slips in practice, they immediately run a "cross country" around the baseball diamond and football practice fields. It is well over a half-mile run. If a coach cusses in practice, he will run his cross country after practice. Of course, the players have the right to remind a coach that he owes the team a lap. Needless to say, I don't think foul language has any place in athletics and it almost never happens in our program.

Over the years, I have heard some awesome testimonies of faith from our seniors. On one of the walls in our locker room, a senior from a few years ago painted a cross with the verse from Philippians 4:13, "We can do all things through Jesus Christ who strengthens us."

Most of our players believe this from the bottom of their hearts. Every Friday night, we tell them to "Take God with you on every play." We advise them to say a quick prayer before every play and tell them not to ask for victory — because I don't really think God cares who wins football games. But I do think he cares that we make a real effort every day to make the most out of the gifts he has given us. We tell them to pray for focus, courage or intensity on that given play.

Before we leave the locker room, we have one final tradition, which is to "Build the Fortress." After we pray as a team, everyone comes together in a tight pack and touches their helmets together overhead. I then recite St. Patrick's prayer and they repeat after me, "Christ behind me, Christ before me, Christ under my feet, Christ beside me, Christ over me, let all around me be Christ." We call this "Building the Fortress" because as we exit the locker room, we feel like one unified army that is invincible if we work together.

During the years that we have been fortunate enough to play in a State Championship game, we have played on Thanksgiving weekend. Without question, my favorite practice of the year is the sharp, tune-up practice we have on Thanksgiving morning. We usually have this practice at an indoor soccer facility where we can get out of the elements and time things up. My favorite part of the practice is at the end when we gather together to pray.

The last thing we do is invite the players to stand and share what it is in their life for which they are thankful. There's always something special about hearing close to one hundred sixteen- and seventeen-year-old young men stand and share with the rest of the group and thank God for the blessings in their lives. I have always wished I could record their words and play them back for their parents. I know it would make them proud and would certainly reinforce that all the sacrifices they have made to send their sons to a Parochial school are well worth it. Likewise, this always reinforces in my mind that I am continuing to live out part of the mission for which I was chosen.

I truly feel blessed to be in a place that allows me the opportunity to share my faith and to help develop young men physically, mentally and spiritually. Heading into the 1999 season, I was fully aware that teaching X's and O's and winning football games was not my primary job. For the rest of my career, my focus would be on fulfilling my part of the Covenant"

Grace

All of this... because of his love for me.

CHAPTER 8

The Perfect Season

People wondered ... were they done winning? Could they compete in 4A? There were many questions to be answered heading into the 1999 season. We had just graduated "The Wolfpack" — without a doubt these guys had been one of the hardest working and most unified groups we have ever had. In addition to being excellent students, they were also outstanding football players. There were several juniors in the class behind them who had contributed during the season, but there were many other pieces of the puzzle that needed to be solved ... people wondered.

A good place to start was with two of our linemen. As a junior, Ryan Brizendine had been an All-State defensive end and had an unbelievable work ethic. Nate Lawrie, a 6' 6" tight end was a straight A student and a major college prospect. We had some very talented players coming back in our "skilled" positions, but most were untested in varsity play. Tommy Schembra, Sean's younger brother, would probably be our starting tailback, but had started as flanker during the previous season. The Schembra brothers were from good bloodlines. Their father Larry was an alumni and had played running back for the school in the late 1960's. Their mother Kathy was also a Roncalli alumnus and a member of the Nalley family — her brother Dick Nalley had been my nemesis while I played at Butler. Kathy has been the varsity volleyball coach at Roncalli for many years and with two state championships of her own is a tremendous competitor. That quality seems to run in the family.

Although he had never taken a varsity snap, Mike Hyde was an outstanding athlete who would probably be our starting quarterback. Mike had missed his junior season due to injury. His father Dan had been an assistant coach at Franklin Central during their championships in the 1980's and 1990's and, coincidentally, had coached at Roncalli in 1993 and 1994. Elijah Hammans, who had been a good receiver at Scecina the previous year, had moved south with his family prior to his senior year and was enrolled at Roncalli. Again, he was a relatively untested player who seemed to have a lot of talent. It appeared that many pieces of the puzzle were available, but putting them together correctly would be a challenge.

Another concern with this group was the team chemistry they had developed. Following the Wolfpack, this group seemed to have a multitude of personalities. Getting them all to pull together to play as one unit would be the last and most important piece of the puzzle. The "Rebelympics" and the accompanying activities seemed to be a good time to work on this. As our players were competing in the events along with their small groups, I had one of our assistant coaches sneak back in the woods next to the game field to build a large bonfire. On a sheet of paper, I had typed in bold capital letters the words SELF-ISHNESS and EGOTISM along with the definitions. I then ran off enough copies to give one to each player. After all the events were finished, we walked the team into the woods to the bonfire, which was quite large by this time and gave one of the papers to each player. I began speaking about selfishness and egotism, and the negative affect these things can have on a team.

I told them I felt these would be our two toughest opponents in the upcoming season. I had intended to get through my talk, then invite everyone who was willing to eliminate selfishness and egotism from the team to throw their sheets on the fire. However, as I mentioned that these were two things that could keep us from a championship, David Moore, who was one of the strongest players we have ever had and a senior co-captain, wadded up his sheet and threw it on the fire. Within seconds, all ninety players had done the same and the effect was inspiring. Suddenly, the flames and the glow from the fire had intensified tremendously. The fact that they had chosen to throw their papers onto the fire before I was able to invite them to do so made it even better. We all stood in silence for a couple of minutes until the flames returned to normal and relished the symbolism of sending our two mortal enemies up in smoke.

By this time, it was almost 1:30 in the morning. I led them in silence to the spot where I had buried the "time capsule" five years earlier. I made a big X on the ground with spray paint and handed a shovel to one of our captains. I told them there were some voices from the past who needed to speak to us and we were going to dig them up. After we unearthed the container, the first letter I pulled out was from Jeremy Stahley, our proud linebacker who was a co-captain of the 1994 State Championship team. Jeremy's younger brother, Jimmy, was a senior on the '99 team and was just as proud and tough as his older brother. Under the moonlight, with only one flashlight to see the pages, I had Jimmy read the letter his older brother had written years before. With a great deal of courage and several pauses to collect his emotions, Jimmy got through the letter. I then had the other seniors read the rest of the letters to the group — matching up brothers or cousins whenever possible.

As the last letter was read, it was apparent that our players suddenly had a new-found appreciation for what tradition really meant. The letters spoke profoundly to them. They emphasized going beyond playing the game to impress the girls or to get their names in the newspaper. They related that it was about bringing pride and honor to family, their teammates and the entire school community. It meant doing everything possible, within the rules, to carry on the legacy of all the fine men who had gone before — players who had given their blood and their honor while wearing the same jerseys. Most importantly, the letters related how to make the most of God's gifts and how to play each play like a man in His eyes, because His are the ones that count! As I witnessed this group absorbing each of these concepts, I became confident that the most important piece of this team's puzzle was falling into place. If the chemistry of this group was strong, everything else would take care of itself during the season. At the conclusion of our Rebelympics, I was confident that this team was ready to begin two-a-day practices and the 1999 season.

The four captains selected by their teammates were David Moore, Ryan Brizendine, Greg Armbruster and Tony Hollowell. Greg was a starting inside linebacker for us and the younger brother of David Armbruster, who had been an All-State tackle for us two years earlier. Tony was the third Hollowell boy to play for us and, at 5' 6" 140 lbs., was the smallest of their clan. But he was tenacious and had a huge heart. So when he was selected as one of the co-captains by his teammates, no one was surprised. We knew these four young men were fine players and would be outstanding leaders for the team.

We started the season against Center Grove, a strong 5A opponent with an enrollment about twice our size. This opening game was played in the RCA Dome, the home field of the Indianapolis Colts and the facility where the State Championship games are played. We emphasized to our players the goal of playing both our first and last games of the season at the Dome. In a very hard-fought game, we pulled away in the second half to secure a 21-7 victory. Elijah Hammans proved his abilities as he hauled in two interceptions and had a couple of key receptions as our flanker. The next week we played very well and defeated Franklin Central 27-0.

In week three, we played Chatard, a rival Catholic school that is always very tough and this proved to be a very strategic game for us. Going into the Chatard game, we knew we would be playing Cincinnati Moeller the following week. We had never played Moeller before but knew they were one of the most storied high school programs in the Midwest, if not the country. We were aware that they would be relying heavily on the scouting report from our game with Chatard and our game plan was to be as basic as possible — sticking with a two tight end offense and a very "vanilla" defense throughout the game. We slugged it out and secured an unimpressive 12-0 victory.

The parents of one of our players happened to be sitting behind the Moeller scouts during the game and related to us that they were visibly unimpressed. In fact, their coaches got up and left at the start of the fourth quarter and our "informant" parents reported hearing one of these guys say, "If this is championship football in Indiana, it's pretty sad!"

In all fairness to them, we didn't look intimidating in the least. On the other hand, just the reverse was true of their team. Heading into our fourth game, Moeller was undefeated — what's more they hadn't been scored on all season and were ranked tenth in the nation by *USA Today*. One of their tackles was Mike Munoz, the 6' 7", 300-lb. son of Anthony Munoz, the NFL Pro Bowl lineman — who many say might be the best lineman to ever play the game. On tape, his son didn't look like he was too far behind him, and Anthony was helping out as an assistant coach with the team. To make matters worse, we had to travel to Moeller to play the game. The odds-makers were not on our side.

As we arrived for pre-game, I was impressed at how focused our players seemed to be as they walked around the huge stadium. This focus and confidence paid off once the game began. We took the opening kickoff, marched the length of the field but had to settle for a field goal when our offense finally stalled around the 15 yard line. But the 3-point field goal was a huge boost to our confidence because we had scored the first points against Moeller up to that point in the season. They answered nicely as they pieced together a time-consuming drive that resulted in a touchdown and a 7-3 lead. On our next drive, we had to rely on some trickery to put points on the board. Mike Hyde threw what appeared to be a screen pass to the left to Mike Williams, who was an All-State punter and our starting free safety. Mike gathered in the pass, paused for a second, then threw a perfect strike about 40 yards downfield to Tommy Schembra, who had lined up at flanker and ran a corner route to the opposite side of the field. The "double-pass" successfully gave us a 10-7 lead.

After exchanging punts, Moeller again sustained a long drive, eventually punching it in to give them a 14-10 lead. Our kids battled every down. With about three minutes to go in the first half, Mike Hyde was instrumental in leading us down the field. Mike was a straight A student, an outstanding athlete and a tremendous competitor. He had played running back in grade school. So, when he dropped back to pass, he was equally as threatening to either throw or scramble with the ball. Against the tenth ranked team in the nation, he did both masterfully. With less than a minute to play in the half, Mike began to scramble, then hit Elijah Hammans on a post pattern over the middle for the score. We were ecstatic to be taking a 17-14 lead at the half.

Both teams made defensive adjustments at halftime and both offenses struggled to put together long drives in the second half. Late in the third quarter, after Ryan Brizendine blocked a Moeller field goal attempt, Elijah Hammans scooped up the ball and returned it deep into Moeller territory. After fighting for every yard, we eventually kicked a field goal to take a 20-14 lead. Again, Moeller answered with a long scoring drive, kicking the PAT to reestablish the lead at 21-20 with about six minutes to go in the game. During the game, we had used about every formation and trick play in our playbook. Since Moeller had never played us before, and had only seen conservative play-calling on the two game tapes we exchanged, we caught them a little off-guard.

Five of the six trick plays we called worked to perfection

and had been instrumental in keeping us in the game. We continued to use different formations and motion as we put together one last drive. With just under two minutes to play, out of trips formation, Hyde hit Schembra in the corner of the end zone for a 26-21 lead. The Roncalli fans erupted into a huge roar of support — sensing that a significant upset was about to take place. Again, not many people had given us much of a chance to beat a team that was ranked in the top ten in the nation. At this point, with their winning tradition behind them, we knew Moeller wasn't about to lay down and die. With less than two-minutes to play, they executed their two-minute offense to perfection as they marched down the field. With the ball on our 4-yard line and facing third down with thirteen seconds on the clock, their quarterback dropped back to pass. Facing immediate pressure, he was forced to unload the pass out in the flats, which fell incomplete.

On fourth down, still on our 4 yard line with less than ten seconds on the clock, their quarterback took a quick three-step drop looking to throw a quick slant to the wide receiver to his right. Our defensive end to that side was Chris Eckhart, a 6' 3" junior. His older brother, Steve, had been an All-State linebacker for us the year before and his oldest brother Joe had been a two-way starter on the '95 team. As the youngest of these three brothers, Chris was a competitor, a tough kid from a tough family. As the ball left the quarterback's hand, Chris leapt high with both hands in the air to bat down the pass. With only four seconds on the clock and Moeller out of timeouts, Mike Hyde took a knee to end the game at our 4 yard line.

As literally thousands of Roncalli faithful emptied the stands to join the on-field celebration, the magnitude of this victory was stunning. Roncalli, a medium-sized school from Indiana, had just beaten the tenth ranked team in the country on their home field. There certainly was cause for celebration! I would say in my twenty-five years of coaching high school football, I have never been involved in a victory where we were so physically outmatched and unquestionably the underdogs. This was also a great lesson to our team that when you work hard, make big plays and stay together as a team anything is possible!

The next week, we had a convincing win over Scecina, but really struggled the week after that as we narrowly pulled out a 13-6 victory over Zionsville. We have always had highly competitive games with Zionsville but this game exposed some weaknesses in both our offensive and defensive personnel. We made three or four player position changes after this game, hoping to get our team ready for playoffs. Our gamble apparently paid off since we won our last three regular season games by an overall score of 148-17. We were pleased that this group seemed very poised and prepared to begin the tournament run.

After a 49-13 win in the sectional opener, we faced Chatard again, whom we had beaten 12-0 the week prior to Moeller. This time, it was "no holds barred" as we played a nearly flawless game to win 31-3. That was the widest margin of victory Roncalli has ever had over a Chatard team. The following week we also won in convincing fashion, 41-8 over Beech Grove. However, winning the sectional championship wouldn't come without a price. Tommy Schembra, our starting tailback, went down early in the second half with a knee injury. Although it wasn't a serious injury, the team doctor said he would be hobbling for the next week or two. Richie Nalley, Tommy's cousin and the son of Dick Nalley, was our backup tailback. Where Tommy was quick and elusive, Richie was more of a power runner who really relished an opportunity to run over opposing players. His style of running served us well as we beat a strong Mt. Vernon team in the Regionals, 27-6. This victory earned us the right to play a very good Whiteland team on their home field in the Semi-State game.

The weather turned bad during Semi-State week. It rained for a good part of the week and continued to rain on game day. Even though Tommy was making progress in his healing, he wasn't back to one-hundred percent yet. Richie would continue to be the "go to" guy on the muddy field at Whiteland. We had the ball first in a driving rain and started out shaky. On our opening drive, we threw an interception that Whiteland returned to our 3 yard line. They pounded in a score a couple of plays later to take a 7-0 lead early in the first quarter. At this point, both our offense and defense really went to work. With Richie repeatedly slamming up the middle or off-tackle with our power toss series, we ate up a lot of clock and ultimately pieced together several long scoring drives. By late in the game, we had put 34 points on the board before we surrendered one last touchdown — making the final score 34-14.

With that victory, I became the first football coach in the state of Indiana to win 100 games in his first ten years as a head coach. Although I think a couple of coaches have done it since then, I was very honored to be the first. More importantly, however, this team was 14-0 and had earned the right to compete for a state title Thanksgiving weekend in the RCA Dome. Our dream of being able to play our first and last game of the season in the Dome had become a reality!

Our opponent in the Championship game would be a very tough team from Norwell. They had a set of twin brothers who were running backs and linebackers. Both were very tough, fast and truly outstanding players. Their quarterback had an excellent arm and behind a big line, their offense had accumulated a lot of points over the season. Their defense was fast, aggressive and very effective. From film, we could tell this was the best team we had faced all year — with the exception of Moeller.

During the first half, Norwell did a great job of controlling both the clock and field position. Those are two aspects of the game we want to control. Through error-free football, Norwell took a 14-10 lead into halftime. Coach Gatts, our defensive coordinator, made some excellent adjustments at the half and Tim Puntarelli, our quarterback coach, had several good ideas about how to shake some receivers free for a potential big play. Coaches and players alike agreed that we had worked too hard and had come too far to have our perfect season blemished. Finishing the season in second place was not an option.

As the second half started, we stormed onto the field with a new resolve. I recall that this group was very prayerful. This was the team who had painted the cross on the locker room wall with the verse "We can do all things through Jesus Christ who strengthens us." As I stated before, we tell our players all the time to "take God with you on every play." As much as any team I have coached, I think this team took both of these thoughts to heart. In the second half, our prayers, our resolve and our undefeated season would be on the line.

Our defense became very stingy, forcing Norwell to punt repeatedly, as we gained control of field position. Elijah Hammans had a couple of nice runs on reverses, which, offensively, complemented our power running game. Coach Puntarelli's plan was to motion our tailback out to trips to put him in single coverage with a linebacker, then hit him over the middle on a post pattern. The plan worked to perfection. Mike Hyde threw a flawless pass to Tommy Schembra, who out-ran the linebacker for a 60-yard score and a 17-14 lead late in the third quarter.

Mike Williams, our free safety, set two State-game records with a 69-yard punt in the second half and, with about five minutes left in the game, returned an interception 50 yards into Norwell territory. Using an unbalanced set and our power toss series, Tommy scored late in the game to make the final score 24-14. We finished the season 15-0 as undefeated State Champions.

I called this chapter "The Perfect Season" but the title is a reflection of more than just an unblemished record. Prior to the season, there had been concerns about dissension and team chemistry. The symbolism of sending selfishness and egotism up in smoke during the Rebelympics stayed with this group. The devout faith this team took into every game helped create an unbreakable bond. Likewise, the trust and friendship among our coaches was stronger than ever. It truly had been a "perfect" season.

As I reflected on the decade of the 1990's and my first ten years as a head coach, I finally felt that we had progressed beyond simply having good teams. I firmly believed we were on the verge of creating a great program. One that would perpetuate itself and continue to grow stronger with time. Most importantly, I wanted our football program to be a four-year experience that would change the lives of our young men and help them grow to be the person God created them to be. I felt this season was a big step in that direction. Some of those who wondered about us early may have received an answer.

Maybe no one would wonder anymore.

CHAPTER 9

The Art of War

Football coaches are crazy. I'm not ashamed to say that and, for the most part, I agree with the statement. But it deserves clarification as to why it's true, why coaches make the strategic decisions they do and, finally, why I choose to stay in the coaching profession amidst all the insanity!

On Friday nights in the fall, thousands of people pack the stands expecting to witness weekly displays of sheer coaching genius. However, problems occur. Every twenty-five seconds, the coach is depending on a group of sixteen- and seventeen-year-old young men to show those thousands of people just how smart he really is. I can't think of another profession in which highly educated adults, many of whom have advanced degrees, put themselves in this situation. It's also common to hear in high school athletics that when you win, the kids did a great job. Conversely, when you lose, the coach really messed things up. Although every coach does "mess up" from time to time, I can honestly say I have never seen a coach miss a tackle, fumble the ball, throw an interception, foul up a blocking assignment or snap the ball on the wrong count.

Over the years, I have come to the stark realization that, as a coach, it is impossible to make everyone happy. We have worked hard to make football a meaningful and worthwhile experience for our players. Consequently, we average over ninety players each season on our varsity roster — and this doesn't include freshman players. I'm proud that we have these numbers and that so many fine young men want to be a part of our program. At the same time, since a team can only have eleven players on the field on any given play, approximately eighty young men are standing on the sidelines anxiously awaiting a chance to perform. Many of these players were the leading rushers, scorers, tacklers or the starting quarterbacks on their grade school teams. And just as anxiously as their sons, there are eighty sets of parents waiting to see their pride and joy get a chance to show what he can do. This is problematic.

The nature of the game of football doesn't help matters. I can't think of another sport where the coach's decision-making skills are placed under such scrutiny. Every twenty-five seconds, a decision must be made and after the play is finished, spectators decide whether or not it was a "good" call. Even when a series of good calls allows the team to march down the field, there tends to be scrutiny. The father of the left tackle is wondering why you aren't running more behind his son because everyone can see that he's dominating the guy across from him. The wide receiver's uncle wishes you would "just throw the streak," because his nephew would "burn him every time." The fullback's brother knows that the trap is the best play in football — especially when his sibling is carrying the ball. The tight end's grandpa would love to see that little "pop pass" right over the middle, while the flanker's mom wonders why the coach never sends her son around on the reverse. And, of course, any time a running play doesn't gain at least 6 yards, the quarterback's Aunt LuLu is yelling, "C'mon, Coach! Throw the ball!" at the top of her lungs.

Most people never question defensive strategy. When the opposing team is moving the ball, the phrase, "C'mon … tackle 'em!!" seems to suffice, because not many can distinguish the 5-2 from the 4-3 package, and even fewer can comprehend the secondary coverage. Many might not even know what the secondary is. Nonetheless, almost everyone in the stands has an opinion about how to run an offense. Ah … the joys of being the offensive coordinator on a Friday night!

Now that I've finished my twenty-fifth year of coaching high school football, I'm much more comfortable with understanding and accepting the dynamics of spectator scrutiny. However, as in most aspects of life, there are a handful of individuals who carry this to an extreme and end up bringing almost as much embarrassment to others as they bring to themselves. I've developed a theory of how this works — complete with an intricate equation (Einstein would be proud.) I call it my Football Intelligence Equation (or FIE.) Here's how it functions:

$$YP + YC - BC = FI$$

With this simple, yet ingenious equation, you can quickly calculate what the Football Intelligence level is of that obnoxious guy (or gal) who keeps standing up during the course of a game to yell their negative comments down at the coaches or players as loudly as possible. The YP stands for "years played" by that person at the high school level and beyond. YC represents "years coached" — again, at the high school level and beyond.

For example, let's say the obnoxious guy up in the stands played football during his freshman and sophomore years of high school. His YP factor would be 2. Then, add this number to his YC factor (number of years he's coached at the high school level.) Since most people have never coached high school football, his YC factor would be zero. This would make his YP + YC factor a 2. Finally, we have to take his BC factor into account and subtract it from the equation. By the way, BC stands for "beers consumed." So, let's assume this fine gentleman guzzles a six-pack of Budweiser before the game. His Football Intelligence Equation would look like this: $YP (2) + YC (0) - BC (6) = FI (-4)$.

This simple equation makes it easy to understand why this person is so willing to stand up in front of hundreds of people and create an embarrassing scene. However, once his FIE gets below a certain level, he probably doesn't even recognize that he's embarrassing himself. It's at this point that he becomes a charter member of the "NEG FIE" Club. This stands for Negative Football Intelligence Equation — meaning he spends an increasing amount of time below the zero point.

Given this, I need to clarify: I have no desire to be demeaning in any way to those with low FIE scores. Actually, the vast majority of people in the stands will have a low score because most haven't played or coached high school football. This is nothing to be ashamed of either. Furthermore, I want to emphasize something I've said publicly many times, Roncalli has the best fans in the state. Our fans pack into our stadium on Friday nights and ninety-nine percent of them are loyal, enthusiastic and supportive. I remind our players constantly how lucky we are to have the love and support of our fans. As I said before, I appreciate the nature of the game — where on any given play there will be differing opinions on what should be called. All of these things are what makes the game so interesting.

The difference is that most folks have enough class, character and integrity to know better than to try to humiliate other people in front of a large crowd. The interesting thing about this is that, as a player or coach on the field, it's impossible to hear individual voices up in the stands. So, insults that are hurled towards the field are seldom heard by the players or coaches. Sadly, many of these comments are heard by the families of the coaches and players, who deserve better than this. Unfortunately, the NEG FIE club members don't seem to care. I'm quite confident medical research would show that these charter club members have an unfortunate deficiency. The resulting void occurs in the part of the brain that controls a very basic thought process. It's called human decency.

I'd like to share another, rather interesting, observation on this point. Almost without exception, those with the highest FIE scores in the stands are the ones who are least likely to cause a scene or make fools out of themselves. This isn't to say they will always agree with play calling or game strategy. Again, it's the nature of football and everyone is entitled to their opinion. But, someone who played high school or college football will have been exposed to the more advanced techniques, terminology and strategies of the game. Those who have high school coaching experience have "been there" and will have a better understanding and appreciation for the intricacies of the game at the high school level, as well as the effort involved in game planning. I put the most stock in the opinions these people have about the game and, normally, they would be least likely to have a desire to embarrass someone else from up in the stands.

NFL football is a marvelous thing. Unfortunately, some people watch just enough to feel confident about their ability to break down and analyze the intricate details of the game of football. This is analogically akin to someone watching the proceedings in a courtroom and then standing to shout instructions to one of the attorneys on legal tactics. As the bailiff escorts the person out of the room, he would likely turn to the crowd and shout, "You need to listen to me. I've seen every episode of 'Matlock' and I watch 'Judge Judy' every week!" Hmmm ... as I think about it, having Football Bailiffs up in the stands on Friday nights might not be a bad idea. However, the NEG FIE club would soon go out of business — which might not be a bad idea either. There. Now I feel better. Those few moments of verbal retaliation were quite gratifying. Now I'm ready to get on with the rest of the book.

I called this chapter "The Art of War" which comes from a book written 2,500 years ago by Sun Tzu, a famous Chinese general. For hundreds of years, his teachings have been used by military personnel, political leaders and business strategists as a guideline on how to run an organization with discipline and sound fundamentals. I believe these principles can also be applied to achieve success in athletics.

In one chapter, Tzu states, "Now the general who wins a battle makes many calculations in his temple ere the battle is fought. The general who loses a battle makes but few calculations beforehand. Thus do many calculations lead to victory, and few calculations to defeat: how much more no calculation at all! It is by attention to this point that I can foresee who is likely to win or lose."

I have no doubt Mr. Tzu would have made a fine football coach. In fact, the ancient Chinese were notorious for their ardent training of soldiers in preparation for war. Obviously, intensive training was part of their pre-war calculations.

Likewise, pre-season training has become crucial to high school athletics. We encourage our athletes to play multiple sports. I was a three-sport athlete in high school and am not keen on focusing on one sport. However, I firmly believe if an athlete isn't actively participating in a sport, they had better have themselves in the weight room — working on getting bigger, stronger and faster. If they don't, they will certainly be passed up by others. This becomes part of the "pre-war" preparation.

Sun Tzu specifically spoke quite a bit about strategy, or calculations. A focal point was to always outnumber your opponent at the point of the attack. His second principle was to outflank your opponent — attacking their weakness. When they adjust their troops to bolster the flank, use deception to attack elsewhere. In other words, the misdirection play, where you fake one way but attack somewhere else. Quite frankly, these are the three main offensive strategies I espouse as well — outnumber, outflank and deceive. Since aircraft wasn't available 2,500 years ago, Sun Tzu was obviously limited as far as an aerial assault was concerned. As I mentioned earlier, I think Sun Tzu would have made a fine football coach — especially in the mud, snow or freezing rains that are common during the final weeks of an Indiana high school football tournament.

The general who calculates the most increases his odds of winning the battle. As a high school and college player, I had no clue how much work and film dissection went into game preparation. For most coaches, eighty-hour work weeks are the norm throughout the fall. Often times, after Jackie and the kids have gone to sleep, I will pop a tape in to do my calculations. Only after extensive film breakdown do you get a real sense of the opponent's tendencies.

There are dozens of considerations we make for our offense each week. Obviously, defensive game planning is just as intricate. If the coach doesn't "make many calculations in his temple ere the battle is fought," his odds of winning are decreased.

I try to have all of the major decisions made before the game begins. Hopefully, we will have rehearsed these situations adequately during practice. Our coaches talk about the "seven-second" rule. As soon as the ball is set, a number of things have to happen in a very short period of time. The coach must recognize which hash the ball is on, and what the down and distance are. At the same time, they must flip through the catalog in their mind or on their clipboard, determine what the opponents tendencies are in this situation and where their best players are likely to be aligned. Next, the coach must give the formation, play and the direction they want the play run to a receiver, who will take it in to the quarterback. In total, you have twenty-five seconds to get your players to the line, set and snap the ball. Therefore, all of these things must be accomplished within about seven seconds or the play won't be sent into the huddle quickly enough to get the play off.

Over the years, the majority of our timeouts have occurred because we were getting too far past the seven second point in a tight situation. Although I'm sure there are fans who disagree with this concept, when we are at a crucial point in the game, I would much rather take a time out to make sure we have the right personnel in the game and call the best play possible for that particular situation than to end up punting the ball away.

There are two basic coaching philosophies that apply to offensive football — the Chess Match and the Fireworks Display. The fireworks-oriented offenses are most likely to draw the oooh's and ahhh's from the crowd. Quite frankly, many times, these teams are more fun to watch and are probably more appreciated by the fans. Conversely, the chess match offense is more patient and strategic — relying mostly on 4-yard gains to systematically move the ball down the field.

Obviously, most people would rather watch a fireworks display than a chess match. Yet, in spite of the quick-score potential of a fireworks offense, I noticed early in my coaching career that in the state of Indiana — with it's unpredictable fall weather — the chess match teams were more likely to play for state championships on Thanksgiving weekend. Therefore, I decided early on that success in the playoffs would certainly override any desire to make our fans say oooh and ahhh due to my spectacular play calling.

Before the 2001 football season, we were bumped back up into class 4A, the second largest class in Indiana. The year before, we had made it to the semi-state game before losing to the eventual state champ. When we made the jump to 4A, some people began to comment that with our outdated offense, we would never be able to compete in that class of football. In 2001, we lost to Cathedral (our archrivals) in overtime during the sectional finals. However, after losing during our first season in 4A (and using that same "outdated" playbook), we've won the past three consecutive 4A State Championships. How can this be? Furthermore, in each of the past three 5A State Championship games, where the coaching is really supposed to be sophisticated, the 5A winner has thrown the ball even fewer times than we have. Imagine that!

My final thought of this chapter is to answer the question: why do I continue to stay in coaching? When I was first hired as the head coach at Roncalli, Joe Hollowell pointed out to me that due to the nature of the game, no one on the south side of Indianapolis would be second-guessed as much as I would. Throughout the regular season when we have big games and during the entire tournament, I can't sleep well at night and I spend most of my waking hours with my bowels in an uproar. This distress is often accompanied by an ongoing, and sometimes powerful, urge to throw up. Usually, I think I do a pretty good job of appearing collected and serene on the outside. Yet, I know that continued suppression of stress isn't healthy — nor is it medically advised. I must confess that a lot of this misery is self-imposed. However, on Friday nights, I do everything possible to ensure that my family and loved ones aren't embarrassed by a mistake or a poor decision I make, and the ensuing reaction from the stands. Even more than this, I don't want to let our players down. They work so hard to do everything we ask and they deserve only the best. During the tournament, the thought of making a call or a decision that might play a role in bringing the season and the high school careers of our seniors to an end is almost unbearable. This thought is at the core of the stress that each football season brings.

I've had a couple of people who are close to me ask why I choose to continue to coach. They point out that I could follow other career paths that would be less stressful and probably make a lot more money in the process. My answer is usually fairly simple. I'm doing what I truly believe God wants me to be doing at this point in my life. I know I'm blessed to be teaching and coaching at Roncalli High School. This blessing comes with the tremendous responsibility and awesome opportunity of working with some incredible young men from wonderful families. Each day, I'm blessed with a chance to have a positive impact on a young person's life. While coaching strategies and playing time are certainly at risk of being criticized, I hope all of our parents feel I have done a good job helping them raise their sons.

There's a saying that "when you coach a young man, you're also coaching his sons." The "life lessons" that a coach passes on to his players will ultimately be passed on to their sons — often times, for generations to come. I've been entrusted with the opportunity to make a difference in their lives. That is very gratifying. Being perpetually nauseous for four months in the fall sounds insane, and yet the insanity fades when one considers that the end result of being a small, influential part of a young man's maturity and growth is more than a worthwhile enterprise. I don't want to imply that my decision to stay in coaching is strictly about selfless giving. To the contrary, what I have gotten in return during my years of coaching far outweighs any sacrifices I have made and anything I may have given to others.

The craziness indeed has a purpose.

CHAPTER 10

Season of Angels

The phone rang. It woke me from a deep sleep. As I reached to answer it, I glanced at the clock which read 1:09 A.M. Immediately, I wondered who in the world would be calling me at this time of night. On the other end was Ricky Clevenger, one of our players who had just finished his sophomore year. Fighting back tears, he informed me that Jonathan Page, his classmate and one of his best friends, had been in a serious automobile accident. He told me it was pretty bad, and wanted to know if I could come to the hospital to be with the family. I told him I'd be right there. It was Monday, June 3, 2002.

Jonathan was a handsome, witty young man with a wonderful and somewhat mischievous smile. He was the fastest kid in his class and an excellent football player. In fact, the coaching staff was counting on him to be a starter the following season as either a defensive back or a flanker — perhaps even both.

On his freshman team, Jonathan had been the leading ball carrier and was voted co-MVP by his teammates. However, he was one of the few players in our program who hadn't attended one of our southside Catholic grade schools. He had attended Center Grove Middle School, a large school system south of Roncalli. In spite of having a very successful first semester at Roncalli, Jonathan decided to transfer to Center Grove for the start of the second semester. He told me he had just missed his old middle school friends too much. He went on to run track that spring at Center Grove.

The next fall, Jonathan showed up on the third day of two-a-day practices, wanting to know if he could come back to Roncalli and be a part of the team. He stood in front of the squad and explained that as soon as he transferred, he knew he had made a mistake. He realized how much he loved and missed Roncalli football and wanted to know if we would accept him back. I informed him that it wouldn't be easy. Since he had played a spring sport at Center Grove, the transfer back would mean he wouldn't be eligible for varsity play. He could, however, play in the junior varsity games in the upcoming season.

As one of our "scout team" running backs, in practice Jonathan always went hard and took an incredible pounding, and yet he was talented and tough, never complained and never backed down from heavy contact. By season's end, he had won the respect of every player and coach in the program. Since he would be eligible for varsity play the next fall, he had everyone convinced he would be one of our best players in his junior year.

As I arrived at the hospital, several of Jonathan's family and friends were already there. Father Tom Clegg, our school priest, came out and informed me that Jonathan's parents, Scott and Holly Page, were in his room and wanted me to come pray with them. Jonathan was in a coma, had several tubes and wires connected to various parts of his body, and was hooked to a ventilator. After visiting and praying with Scott and Holly, Father Tom gathered several of the football players who were there and recommended we "build the fortress" — like we do before every game by joining hands with Scott and Holly, forming a circle around Jonathan's bed and reciting St. Patrick's prayer. The words "Christ behind me, Christ before me, Christ under my feet, Christ beside me, Christ over me, let all around me be Christ" had never held a stronger meaning or intent. I definitely felt the presence of Jesus in the room that night.

Like a warrior, Jonathan refused to surrender and continued to fight for his life. Living longer than expected, he passed away two days after his accident. As I went to visit the family, Scott asked if Steve Wilson, our head freshman coach and I would do the eulogy. Knowing that it would be one of the most difficult things I have ever done in my coaching career, I replied that I would be honored.

The day before the funeral, calling was held at the Catholic church the family attended to allow Jonathan's many friends and loved ones to pay their respects. As Jackie and I made our way forward, I asked her to kneel and pray with me by the casket. When I gazed at Jonathan's handsome face, I noticed he had a football tucked under his forearm and on his chest was a picture of him carrying the football in a Roncalli game. I was suddenly overcome with emotion and began to weep openly. In the twenty-three years I had known Jackie, this was the only time she had seen me cry. However, I was neither ashamed nor embarrassed. I had grown to love this young man because of his courage, personality and warrior's heart. I could only imagine the heartache his parent's were enduring.

At Jonathan's funeral the next day, the church was full of family and friends who had come to celebrate his life and mourn his passing. As a show of solidarity, players and coaches from Chatard, Cathedral, Scecina and Ritter, all rival Catholic schools, were in attendance. The largest group, other than Roncalli, were the players from Center Grove, who in many instances had known Jonathan since grade school. To further underscore their unity that day all of the players from each of the schools were wearing their jerseys.

Steve Wilson gave his part of the eulogy first and did a wonderful job of paying tribute to Jonathan. As I was approaching the lectern to give my part of the eulogy, I prayed that God would grant me courage to get through it, wisdom to appropriately reflect on Jonathan's life, and enough compassion to let Scott and Holly know how lucky their son was to have them as parents.

I began by thanking all those in attendance, especially the

players and coaches from the other schools. I went on to say there were three things I would always remember about Jonathan. The first was his courage. The resolve he showed in leaving Roncalli, then coming back to receive a tremendous pounding without ever complaining was remarkable. His courage carried over to his time in the hospital as he fought like a warrior for his life. His courage would always be remembered.

The second thing I stated was that I would never forget his mischievous smile and his sense of humor. Beyond his good looks and great athletic talent, he was a wonderful young man. I told Scott and Holly that he was a beautiful reflection of them, and that he knew how much they loved him. Likewise, he loved them very much, was proud to be their son and was lucky to have them as his parents. I asked Scott and Holly to look around the room. The huge crowd was certainly a fine tribute to their son but it was also a true reflection of both of them.

Finally, I would always remember the way Jonathan touched the lives of others. I shared that I had recently grown to believe the ultimate way we can give thanks to God for the countless gifts He has given us is to help bring others closer to Him so we might all experience His life-changing love. I asked those in the church to reflect back on the events of the past week: the prayers sent to God; all of the love and support given to the Page family; and the different school communities that had all come together as one Christian family to honor a wonderful young man and his family. I finished by stating, "If, in fact, the greatest way to pay tribute to God is to use our gifts to bring other people closer to Him, I think this truly is Jonathan's finest hour. Jonathan, we thank you for that!" God had certainly answered my prayers and allowed me to get through the eulogy without breaking down. More importantly, I hope I was able to be a part of helping Scott and Holly give their precious son back to God.

When the funeral concluded, players from all the schools lined both sides of the long sidewalk from the church to the hearse to pay a final tribute to Jonathan as the coffin was carried past. Along with the Page family, I appreciated this show of support and unity from the other schools.

We began the summer mourning Jonathan's death, however, other concerns were being dealt with as well. In the spring of the previous school year, six upcoming seniors had been caught drinking at a party. These six included a few of our better players, some of whom had been projected to be starters. According to school policy, they would all be suspended for the first two and one-half games of the season (twenty-five percent of our regular schedule.) Our first four opponents were extremely tough. So, not having some of our best players available created a significant amount of worry. In addition to our roster problems, we had even more serious concerns since two of our player's fathers were battling cancer and struggling to cling to life.

Karl Andrews had graduated from Roncalli in the late 1970's where he met his lovely wife Robin. Bob Tully coached at Roncalli when Karl played and said he was one of the toughest, most hard-nosed players he's ever coached. Karl was from a family of sixteen kids and had to work very hard to help pay his tuition to Roncalli. He carried the same determined work ethic into his adult life. He was a loving husband to Robin and a wonderful father to his four children. Karl's oldest son, Nick, had played for us on our 1999 State Championship team and possessed many of his father's qualities, and his second son, Phil, was going to be a sophomore on the 2002 squad. Karl had many, many friends and was loved not only by his immediate family, but by all who knew him.

As the summer passed, Karl's health continued to decline. Due to his extreme weight loss and the fact that he felt so poorly, only family members were permitted to see him. On July 23, 2002, he passed away while surrounded by his family. Given his lifelong love and passion for Roncalli football, our program had truly lost a strong member of the Roncalli family. For the second time that summer, our community was in mourning.

Despite the heartbreaking loss of two members of the

Roncalli family, we continued to prepare for the start of the season even with the knowledge that another member of our football family was fighting for his life. Dick Nalley, who had been the toughest college player I had come up against while at Butler was in the final stages of his battle with cancer.

As a running back at Roncalli in the early 1970's, he was the perfect combination of strength, speed, toughness, agility and explosive power. He was named First Team All-State and Catholic All-American. Additionally, he set all of Roncalli's sprint records in track and would go on to set multiple rushing records at Indiana Central University in Indianapolis. After college, he came within 37/100ths of a second from winning the bronze medal in the 1980 Olympics at Lake Placid in the bobsled competition.

From a high school All-American to an Olympic hero, many old timers still say he was the best football player to ever come out of Roncalli. When I became friends with Dick as an adult, what I admired most about him was that he was a wonderful father to his two sons and two daughters. Richie, his oldest son, played a key role as a ball carrier on the 1999 team. He then became our leading rusher and scorer on the 2000 team. Marcus, Dick's younger son, was a three year starter in our varsity backfield, and was our starting tailback on both the 2001 and 2002 teams. Like his father, Marcus was extremely strong, fast and explosive. At 5' 11" and 205 lbs., he ran a 4.55 40-yard dash and could bench press 360 lbs. Just like his father, he relished being a punishing runner.

Twenty-five years earlier, when I was competing against Dick at the collegiate level, I had no idea that his sons and nephews would become All-State running backs on the high school teams I would be coaching. As an athlete and a competitor, Dick always had an indestructible "Superman" persona about him. Even after his days as an Olympic athlete were over, he continued to participate in weightlifting competitions. With a body weight under 200 lbs., he could still bench press well over 400 lbs. and won several state power lifting titles. Even as he approached middle age, he still carried a "larger than life" persona on the south side of Indianapolis.

Throughout the summer of 2002, cancer continued to weaken his once indestructible body. But being a warrior seems to run in the Nalley blood. He lived far beyond what his doctors had projected and made it very clear that one of his primary goals was to see his son play football again. It was a tremendous source of pride for Dick that his sons had followed in his footsteps to become star running backs for Roncalli. Through sheer courage, fortitude and an iron will, he clung to life and was able to see his wish come true.

We opened the 2002 season at Center Grove, a team that has become a 5A powerhouse in Indiana football. Both teams lined up on their respective 45 yard lines before the game. In honor of Jonathan, a tribute was read over the intercom, a few moments of silence were observed and finally several balloons were released. It was a wonderful tribute to Jonathan and a fitting way to start the season.

As the game began, our offense sputtered a bit — because of the suspensions and a couple of injuries among key players. Marcus played his heart out and ultimately scored our only touchdown of the night as we lost our hard fought season opener 14-7. After the game, I was in the press box waiting for the postgame radio interview, when I saw three or four men slowly moving down the steps. After a closer look, I could see they were huddled around Dick, who was carefully making his way out of the stadium. Since I hadn't seen him for a few weeks, I was shocked at how thin and frail he seemed. At the time, it didn't occur to me that this would be the last time I would see him inside a football stadium.

The next week, we prepared for our game against Franklin Central and I knew we were going to have our hands full. On film, this team reminded me a lot of the 1990 team coached by Chuck Stevens. Even though Marcus didn't want to talk about his dad's health, I had heard Dick was getting steadily worse. However, since it was one of his father's strictest rules, Marcus never missed practice. That Wednesday night, early in practice, Marcus' brother, Richie, pulled up to the practice field. I was at the far end of the field and didn't get to speak to either of them, but they both got in the car and left in a hurry. After practice that evening, we were notified that Dick had passed away. In less than three months, the Roncalli community would be burying another beloved member of our family.

When Marcus returned to school on Friday, there wasn't a moment's doubt whether he would be playing in the game that evening. Dick would have insisted that he not miss the game. That morning, Marcus came to see me to ask about changing his jersey number. In high school, he had always worn number 30 while his dad had worn 24 in high school and college. Marcus said, "Coach, I've never wanted to wear my father's number because I wanted to create my own identity and not play in his footsteps. Now, I want that to change. I want to run exactly in my father's footsteps to honor him. Can I switch my jersey number to 24?" At that point, he was doing a much better job keeping his eyes from welling up with tears than I was.

Wearing number 24 that night, Marcus ran like a man possessed. Due to the ongoing player suspensions, we were outmatched up front and there was often nowhere to run. It was obvious, however, that Marcus was consumed with passion as he once again scored our only touchdown. We lost again that night, as we would the following week to a very good Chatard team. They scored in the last thirty seconds to win 14-10. In week four, we traveled to Cincinnati to play Elder, a big all-boys Catholic school that went on to win Ohio's largest class state championship that year. They pounded us pretty soundly and, for the first time as either an athlete or coach, I was sitting on a 0-4 record. It became very obvious that death is not a good motivator. Instead, it only serves to drain you — both physically and emotionally.

During the two and a half hour ride home from Cincinnati, I reflected on what this group of young men had dealt with over the previous four months. It occurred to me that our team was at a crossroads, and that our attitude and approach in the upcoming weeks would dictate how the rest of the season would turn out. I also knew that ultimately it was my responsibility to redirect this ship which was adrift.

Since it was almost 2:00 in the morning by the time we had the buses unloaded and everyone gathered in the locker room, I decided to make my post-game remarks short and to the point. I said, "Fellas, right now, we are 0-4. Obviously, we have a lot of work to do. But, I've been around you long enough to know something about your character and I know the families you come from! Seniors, I'm telling you right now, you will not lose another game in your high school football careers!" As the seniors made quick, sideways glances at each other, a look of determination and commitment occupied their faces. This resolve was exactly what we needed. I pulled them together for the closing prayer then sent them home.

I wasn't surprised when the team came out fired up for practice the next week. After a disappointing 0-4 start, unlike most groups, these guys were hitting and hustling with a vengeance. Adding fuel to the fire was the fact that we were to play Scecina on our home turf that week. We all knew we were in desperate need of a win, and this team felt a victory over a rival Catholic school at home could be the turning point in our season. When the school day began that Friday, they were chomping at the bit to play!

By lunch time, however, we were beginning to receive reports that a nasty storm was heading our way. The storm was heading for Indianapolis from the southwest and was bringing various tornado watches and warnings along with it. By 1:00, the sky had taken on an ominous appearance and the area was placed under a tornado watch. At 1:45, we were informed that a tornado had touched down and was heading directly towards

BEYOND THE GOAL LINE

the southeast side of the city, which meant Roncalli was in it's path. We were also warned that it would arrive in the next fifteen minutes. In keeping with our emergency plans, we immediately gathered all 1,000 students, faculty and staff into the lower and middle hallways, and closed every door in the building.

By 2:00, the wind was blowing so hard I was afraid the walls might collapse. Thankfully, within ten minutes, it had passed. Although we usually dismiss students for the day at 3:00, the state police called to let us know that a tornado had indeed passed through the neighborhood. We were told that area homes had been destroyed and power lines were down everywhere. The police also let us know that we should keep everyone in the building until some roadways could be cleared. Approximately three hours later, we were finally allowed to dismiss the students. The city was beleaguered; businesses were closed, transportation was impossible and people scrambled to salvage what remained. As you may suspect, our game that night was cancelled.

As I walked through the parking lot, the scene around me was surreal. The neighborhood west of the school had been devastated. Large trees were down, entire roofs had been ripped off homes, and furniture and personal belongings were scattered everywhere. Several homes had been completely flattened with no walls standing. I had never seen anything like it before. Later, we found out the tornado had stayed on the ground for 112 miles — the second longest in Indiana history. Miraculously, no one had been killed; however, the damage estimate throughout the area was over $50 million. The only noticeable damage to Roncalli was to two forty foot pine trees, which had been uprooted from the circle at the front of the school. God must have been watching over the inhabitants of our school building that day!

As happy as I was regarding the safety of our school, I was concerned about the psychological state of our football team. We had fought through three devastating deaths, the suspensions of some key players, an 0-4 start and, now, a tornado that cancelled game five. Going into the sixth week of the season, we were still winless. I was beginning to wonder just how much more this team could take.

To my amazement, they came out the following week more focused and energized than ever. They were convincing me they truly had what it takes to be a championship team. That Friday night, we played one of the best games in my career as a coach when we defeated Elkhart Central, a 5A team from northern Indiana, 42-7. Marcus played an unbelievable game and rushed for 327 yards (a new school record) and five touchdowns in less than three quarters of play. After starting 0-4, we won our last four regular season games by a combined score of 180-23.

After a convincing win in the sectional opener, we faced Cathedral on their home field exactly one year after they had beaten us there in overtime to end our season. Just like the year before, it was a classic "slug-fest." Our quarterback, Nick Johnson, hit Marcus out of the backfield for an 18-yard touchdown pass in the first quarter. Cathedral then put together a long scoring drive early in the second quarter to tie the score at 7 each. With the first half winding down, we tried to sustain a drive to put points on the board to hopefully take a lead into halftime.

Earlier that week, I was standing in class when Pat Kuntz, who had been a close friend of Jonathan's, approached me. He asked if it would be okay if he was a little late to practice that day because he and a couple of friends wanted to go to Jonathan's grave after school to commemorate his birthday. Of course, I gave my approval and, as I turned around to the clipboard on my desk, I suddenly felt overwhelmed by a feeling of peacefulness throughout my body. I was drawn to the clipboard and wrote down an unusual unbalanced, shotgun formation with motion that we had never used before. As I look back now, I'm convinced that Jonathan's spirit had visited me and urged me to write down this bizarre formation and accompanying play. I installed the play in practice that week, but had forgotten about it during the game.

Late in the second quarter, in a crucial situation, I felt Jonathan's presence again so I decided to call Jonathan's play. It caught Cathedral by surprise as Marcus took off on a 42-yard gain. This set up a second touchdown for Marcus as we took a 14-7 lead into halftime.

We fought back and forth through the second half until Cathedral finally punched in a score with less than three minutes to play. Their PAT tied the score 14 all. Ironically, this had been the score the previous year on the same field at the end of regulation play. Although I felt prepared, I didn't want to go into overtime again — at this point, the momentum was on their side.

Starting with the ball on our 27 yard line with about 2 and a half minutes to play, I was hoping just to move the ball systematically down the field to set up a field goal. Instead, with about two minutes to go, Marcus found a slight seam, shot through the hole and outran their defenders for a 66-yard touchdown run. As he crossed the goal line, he looked up and pointed his finger to the sky. Although some in the crowd might have thought he was making the sign for #1, everyone on our side knew to whom he was signaling. After the game, he told his mom that as he broke through the hole, he could see his father standing down past the end zone among the huge crowd. So, he ran right towards him. As he entered the end zone, his father was gone. I have no doubt that Dick's spirit was with Marcus that night as he rushed for 239 yards and scored all three touchdowns against a strong Cathedral defense.

After winning a hard-fought Sectional Championship over Shelbyville, we traveled to a very tough East Central team in the Regional game. As is usual in Indiana in the fall, practice that week was cold and rainy, and the foul weather continued through game night. Even though East Central was a junior dominant team, they were very fast and physical. We took a 10-7 lead into the fourth quarter, but they kicked a field goal late in the game to send it into overtime. By now, the playing conditions were as miserable as any I had ever faced. The cold rain was blowing almost parallel to the ground, cutting like a razor as it hit your skin. Despite the conditions, neither team was ready to let down.

East Central won the coin toss and elected to play defense first. Even with a sore knee, Marcus pounded it in to take a 17-10 lead. East Central then had the ball on the 10 yard line going in and four downs to score. After a couple of unsuccessful runs, their quarterback began to scramble, looking to pass. He threw it out into the flats to his left, but David Oechsle, our outside linebacker, made a diving interception to end the contest and send us to the semi-state game. The overtime loss was heartbreaking for East Central and, since they had so many underclassmen starting, we knew they would be an awesome force to contend with the next season.

At this point, all of our energy had to be focused on getting ready for the upcoming semi-state game in which we would face the mighty Jasper Wildcats. This team was coached by Indiana's all-time winningest coach, Jerry Brewer, who was finishing a brilliant forty-four-year career. His 368 wins were the most in Indiana history. The previous year, he led Jasper to the 4A State Championship (his first as a head coach.) Therefore, his team was determined to make it two in a row. Before the season began, Jerry announced that he would retire at the end of the season — win or lose. Obviously, we knew his team was going to come into our place sky high and that it would be a very emotional game for both teams.

The offensive strategy of both schools was almost identical: power football out of the "I" backfield and a lot of power toss. Three of their most highly skilled players were brothers — the quarterback and wide receiver were identical twins, who were really fast and, as seniors, were a dangerous combination. Their younger brother was the tailback. Like Roncalli, their offense was very physical and run-oriented — as most teams still playing at this point of the Indiana tournament are.

That night, Roncalli proved to be a little more durable as we rushed 64 times for 240 yards compared to 25 Jasper attempts for 131 yards. Phil Gatts had retired from coaching varsity football after the 2000 season to spend more time with his family. After his many years of loyal service, he deserved a break. Chris Belch became our new defensive coordinator. He had played at Roncalli in the mid-1980's under Bill Kuntz and lived and breathed Roncalli football. Chris and our defensive staff did a masterful job preparing for Jasper's offense, holding them to six points. Marcus scored in the third quarter, followed by a Kevin Trulock field goal. At least half a dozen times in the third quarter, Marcus pounded ahead on third and short, or fourth and short, to pick up the first down by inches. His efforts allowed us to eat up the clock and barely hold on to a narrow 10-6 victory. Marcus certainly earned his keep that night with 50 carries (a new Roncalli record) and 179 yards rushing.

Interestingly, I had felt the distinct presence of our three angels prior to the game. It had rained just about every night that week and, in an attempt to keep the field as dry as possible, we had put down several sheets of plastic every night after practice. Unfortunately, the plastic needed to be removed each day to allow the grass to "breathe." All week long, I spent my prep periods removing plastic — only to repeat the process the next day. This daily chore made me lose a lot of valuable game preparation time. When we cleared the plastic off for the last time on game day, I realized I was less prepared for this game mentally and organizationally than I had been for any game in my coaching career. The game field looked nice but, psychologically, I was a mess. Here I was getting ready to play against the defending State Champions and I was hopelessly unprepared.

About ninety minutes before game time, I felt like I was on the verge of having an anxiety attack. As I opened the door to my office, I noticed a large sign on the wall that I hadn't seen all week. In big, bold letters, it read, "WE ARE GUIDED BY ANGELS," followed by "24, 26, 31" — which had been Dick,

Jonathan and Karl's jersey numbers. Suddenly, I felt the familiar warm, tingling sensation engulf my body. My heart rate immediately began to return to normal and, for the first time all week, I actually felt calm and at peace. The feeling remained with me for the rest of the night — even through the numerous points of the game when our entire season was on the line. To this day, I believe our three angels produced that calm.

Prior to that season, I'm not sure I even believed in angels intervening in human affairs. But now, beyond a shadow of a doubt, I know it is true. In the past three years, I've had several other people share "angel stories" from that season — too many to write about in this book. I know the spirits of Jonathan, Karl and Dick were with us that season.

I had coached in three state championship games prior to 2002, but this was our school's first trip in 4A football. Ft. Wayne Dwenger, our opponent, was big, fast, aggressive and exceptionally well coached. We knew we would have to execute in all three phases of the game to have a shot at winning. Dwenger boasted a 13-1 record compared to our 9-4 season. Interestingly, exactly twenty years earlier, Roncalli had played in the school's first state championship against Dwenger. Steve Wilson, our freshman coach, was the star running back on that Roncalli team. Early in the fourth quarter, Roncalli had held a 21-7 lead but Dwenger came back late in the game to win it 22-21. At our 2002 championship game, there were many former Rebels in the crowd who wanted to even the score. Little did they know that, in many ways, this game would mirror that night twenty years before, with one important twist.

Roncalli opened the game by marching 72 yards on 14 plays, consuming almost seven minutes of the clock. Nick Johnson hit our tight end, Jake McCoy, with a 17-yard touchdown pass to take a 7-0 lead. Midway through the second quarter, Kevin Trulock hit a 36-yard field goal to increase our lead to 10-0. Before the half, Dwenger responded with a 68-yard scoring drive to leave the score 10-7 at the half. In the third quarter,

Dwenger carried their momentum into the opening drive with a 66-yard march down the field to take the lead with a 14-10 score. Our offense began to sputter in the third quarter and things began to look very bleak when Marcus was tackled on the sideline and heard a loud "pop" from his knee. Suddenly, we were faced with going into the fourth quarter without our best player. Marcus had rushed for over 2,300 yards but as of that moment, he was done for the season. We were stunned and heartbroken.

Early in the fourth quarter, Dwenger scored again to take a 21-10 lead. Ironically, the sportswriters had projected us as 11 point underdogs. With Marcus out of the game, it appeared they might be right. What they hadn't taken into account, however, was the warrior mentality of this team. We had fought through so much and the entire team had taken a vow in our locker room at 2:00 A.M. after game four that our seniors weren't going to taste defeat again that season.

We trailed by 11 points with 9:25 left to play when Dwenger punted from mid-field to our 15 yard line. D.J. Russell, our senior wide receiver, fielded the ball and returned it 30 yards to the 45 yard line. We had inserted Tim Sergi, our starting free safety, who was a tall, fast, physical sophomore, as tailback to replace Marcus. I began to pray for focus, clarity and peace of mind, and I think God granted all three. With Marcus out of the game, we went back to "Jonathan's offense," the unbalanced shotgun set with a lot of motion. Nick Johnson did a masterful job running the offense as we combined quick spot passes to Kyle Stephenson, a senior and one of the best athletes on the team, with backs motioning out of the backfield and periodic quarterback draws. Nick was a very deceptive runner on these draws and, after leading us on a 55 yard drive, ended up doing a complete flip in the end zone following a 4-yard run for the score.

With less than six minutes to play, we were trailing 21-17. Our defense really stepped up as Peter Szostak, our defensive end, made two consecutive tackles for a loss, and forced our opponent into a three and out. We returned the punt to mid-field with 4:25 to go. Mixing formations, Tim Sergi ran with poise and determination not usually found in a sophomore — especially not one who had played almost the entire season on the other side of the ball. Facing fourth down and two from the fourteen yard line with under two minutes to play, Tim slammed off left tackle on a toss play to pick up a first down on the five yard line. His adrenaline surged as we gave it to him to the right for another four yard gain. With one minute to play and the ball on the one yard line, we were trailing by four points. The State Championship was on the line and the roar inside the RCA Dome was deafening.

We decided to run a power toss to the left — the weak side of the formation. Tim took the pitch, made one cut and knifed into the end zone! The Rebel crowd went berserk and I don't think I have ever heard a crowd in the dome which was that loud — before or since. Ahead by one, we punched in the two point conversion off right tackle to take a 24-21 lead. Our defense held for four downs and we took a knee to run out the clock. Just as Dwenger had done twenty years earlier, we came from two scores down late in the fourth quarter to claim a state championship. This was the sixth in our school history and my fourth as the head coach.

At Roncalli that evening, we held a standing room only pep session in the gymnasium. After several words of thanks, I called Scott and Holly Page up on stage. I explained that we had kept Jonathan's name and jersey number on our roster for the entire season because we knew he would be there with us in our hearts and souls for the duration of the season. I told them I had no doubt that at that very moment he was watching with that big, handsome smile on his face. I then told them I had a presentation I wanted to make. In a very emotional moment, I removed my state championship medal and placed it around Scott's neck and told him I wanted him to have it on Jonathan's behalf. Afterward, I gave both he and Holly long, heartfelt hugs.

Reflecting back on the 2002 season, I continue to pray for the families of Jonathan, Karl and Dick. I know there is nothing we can ever do to bring back their loved ones. However, if in some small way we allowed others to feel their presence, even for a few fleeting moments, all of our lives are richer because of it. I know their spirits were present in my life frequently during that season and, periodically, I am blessed with their presence yet today.

What continues to ring in my soul now is not the memory of the haunting phone call I received that bleak Monday morning so long ago. What rings now is the peace of knowing that I have been transformed somewhat by the presence of love ... the love that resounds in the joy through Jonathan Page, Karl Andrews and Dick Nalley. Consequently, I know my life will never be the same.

Marcus Nalley crossing the goal line, pointing up to his father, Dick, who had the best seat in the house.

CHAPTER 11

Against All Odds

Roller coasters. In many regards, with their ups and downs, twists and turns, they are just like life. In the mid to latter 1980's, I had no idea that the lives of the three coaches from Lawrence Central (Bob Ashworth, Frank Sergi and Bob Hasty) would later become so entwined with mine. All three ended up living on the south side of Indianapolis and decided to send their sons (Nate Ashworth, Tim Sergi and Andrew Hasty) to Roncalli. The fact that I had the chance to coach all three of these young men on the same team was more than ironic.

They had grown into fine young men and I was genuinely excited that I would have the opportunity to coach them. As a junior on the 2002 State Championship team, Nate had started all season as a middle linebacker and was one of our leading tacklers. At 6' 2" and about 225 lbs., he was clearly the best athlete in his grade. In addition, he was a straight "A" student who was ranked fourth in his class. During his sophomore and junior years, he started on both the varsity football and basketball teams and in the weight room was the strongest returning player on the team. Nate was a handsome young man with a mature, engaging personality and, as a result of his football abilities, was being looked at by some big colleges. He was an inspiring kid from a great family, who certainly had everything going his way. All this would change suddenly on Mother's Day, May 18, 2003.

That morning, Jerre McManama, who coached our running backs, was sitting with his family in church at St. Jude awaiting the start of mass. Nate came in and sat next to Jerre, something he often did. Almost immediately, Jerre noticed that Nate was wearing glasses — something he had seldom seen. He also looked a little disheveled and seemed to be a bit slow and sluggish. At first, Jerre though he might just be feeling under the weather, but when Nate remained seated when the rest of the congregation stood, he became more concerned. As Jerre looked closer, he noticed Nate's eyes were glazed over and he had begun to sweat profusely. Nate was blinking slowly and he was responding a bit incoherently. Jerre helped him to the back of the church to get a drink of water, then assisted him outside for some fresh air and to cool off.

Jerre's mother, who had been sitting with the group, had a medical background and commented to him that it appeared Nate might be having a stroke. Jerre immediately called 911 and paramedics arrived and whisked Nate off to the hospital. Later that day, it was confirmed that he had indeed suffered a stroke. Personally, I had never heard of a healthy seventeen-year-old, who was in phenomenal shape, having a stroke. That this could happen to Nate was certainly a shock to everyone. Beth Ashworth, Nate's mother, is a highly successful heart surgeon in Indianapolis. His father, Bob, had been involved in athletics for his entire life. They both decided they wanted to find the cause of the stroke, so they asked for complete blood tests to check for alcohol or any trace of drugs. Every test came back clean — I would have been absolutely shocked otherwise, Nate had always been about as close to the "All American Kid" as you could get.

For the next several weeks, Nate remained in the hospital. Even though he took his tremendous work ethic and great attitude with him into therapy each day, it became apparent that he was going to face a long road to recovery. It was also determined that he would miss the next school year — both academically and athletically. Since he was the best athlete in his class, we knew we would miss Nate's physical presence on the field. Moreover, we also knew we would miss his great attitude and quiet leadership skills. In yet another ironic twist, when they were freshmen, Nate and Jonathan Page had been voted the co-offensive MVP's — now neither would be able to play their senior season.

The only other seniors who had started the previous year as juniors were Nick Sexton at defensive end, Nick Marshall at flanker and Mark Evans at offensive guard. At 6' 3" and 220 lbs., Nick Sexton had the best chance of being recruited by a bigger school. Unfortunately, early in the second game of the year, he sustained a season-ending ACL injury to his knee, which left Evans and Marshall as the only returning senior starters.

At the start of the season, the team picked David English as a co-captain along with Mark Evans, Nick Marshall and Nate Ashworth. David was 5' 8" and 165 lbs., and was a tenacious player. Although Nate couldn't dress for games and was enrolled in just a couple of classes at school, he went out for pre-game coin tosses and took part in other captain duties. His ongoing courage, determination and positive attitude served as a source of inspiration to us all! With our senior ranks depleted, we certainly needed all the motivation we could get. On paper, this group had the makings of an average to below average team. We went on to lose the first three games — two in blowouts and one on the last play of the game. Sitting on an 0-3 record, with some of our best players on the sidelines, we found ourselves at a crossroads early in the season.

One of the great things about athletics in general, and football in particular, is that on a daily basis, you are given opportunities to learn lessons about yourself.

How committed are you to achieving your goals?

Are you a loyal person and can others count on you when the chips are down?

How do you respond to criticism?

After being knocked down repeatedly, do you continue to

get up each time with even more resolve in your heart that you aren't going to let it happen again?

In short, how do you deal with disappointment and adversity? This is the true test of character. Without a doubt, the 2003 team had to answer these questions — just as they had the year before. Just as our coaches had grown to expect, they answered these questions boldly.

After playing very poorly in game three, we turned the corner in game four by playing very well to secure a solid 44-0 victory. We went on to finish our regular season at 6-3 and outscored our final six opponents by a combined score of 218-27. All three phases of the game were clicking when we won our first two sectional games by a combined total of 52-7. We started the season as a very inexperienced and vulnerable team. Yet, we played our last eight games with a lot of heart, pride and poise. Certainly, this was a reflection of the great character this group possessed. All of these team qualities were going to be put to the test, as well as my own fortitude, as we headed into sectional championship week against Zionsville.

As usual, Zionsville had a well-coached, hard-nosed team. However, their senior class was one of the most physically gifted groups in their school's history. Three years earlier, as freshmen, they had whipped our team 31-7, one of the worst losses our freshman squad had suffered in quite a while. The fact that this thrashing had occurred when Nate Ashworth, Jonathan Page and Nick Sexton were still playing was certainly cause for concern.

To make matters worse, Jackie was admitted to the hospital the previous week for intestinal surgery. She ended up spending ten days there and was mostly bed-ridden. I immediately developed a new-found respect for single parents. I have often said I'm not a great father during football season because of the long hours required. Trying to be both Mom and Dad to four relatively young children during the ten days Jackie was in the hospital was extremely tough — both on me and the kids. Jackie's sister, Jennifer, truly was an angel during our time of need. She helped with cooking, cleaning and homework in Jackie's absence. Likewise, our assistant coaching staff had to pick up the slack to allow me to leave practice early to visit my wife in the hospital. I would then try to get home early enough to help the kids with their homework, clean the kitchen and get the kids ready for bed. Throughout it all, in the back of my mind, I knew an outstanding Zionsville team was looming on the horizon. Needless to say, along with worrying about Jackie, I didn't get much sleep that week! Looking back on it now, I think God was challenging me a little, to see if I could practice what I preach. I'm still not positive but I think I passed the test.

As always, our assistant coaches did a tremendous job preparing the team for the Zionsville game. Our stadium was packed and electricity was in the air at the opening kick-off. Both teams put together sustained drives — ours mostly from the run, Zionsville mostly from the pass. Their quarterback went six out of eight for 132 yards and one touchdown — leading Zionsville to a 14-10 halftime lead. Chris Belch, our defensive coordinator, worked his magic with the defensive scheme during the half, and Brian Lauck tweaked our coverages just enough to create some different looks in the secondary for the second half. Our halftime adjustments proved to be effective and their quarterback was able to complete only one out of seven attempts in the second half.

Conversely, our offense began to move the ball much more effectively in the second half — with our quarterback, Chris Schmaltz, going six out of six for over 100 yards passing and a touchdown. Our running game helped us score twice in the second half. With about six minutes remaining in the fourth quarter, we held a 24-14 lead.

Woody Hayes once said when you throw the ball three things can happen ... and two of them are bad. Unfortunately, the worst of the three took place with about five minutes left in the game. We were at mid-field, protecting a ten point lead, when we called a short pass out in the flats to our fullback. This time the opposing linebacker read it perfectly, stepped in front of the pass and scooted up the sideline for a 50-yard touchdown return. After their kicker, who was outstanding, made the extra point, we suddenly found ourselves holding a very fragile three point lead.

We started our last possession at our own 20 yard line and our kids dug in. We systematically punched the ball down the field until we took a knee inside their 10 yard line to let the clock expire. With the exception of the interception, this team had played one of the best halves of football (against an extraordinary team) I have ever been associated with. I couldn't have been more proud of our kids or our assistant coaching staff. They were supremely prepared, largely in my absence, and had all competed like warriors. Against all odds, we were sectional champions.

We faced a very good Mooresville team on our home field in the Regional the next Friday. Jackie was home from the hospital and although she was very slow getting around for a few days, our family life began to return to normal. Needless to say, we were thrilled to have her home. With normalcy also returning to our practice routine, we had a great week of preparation for our match against Mooresville. On game night, however, they took their first possession right down the field for a score and quickly gained a 7-0 lead. Our offense responded by playing one of the best games we played all year. Tim Sergi, our tailback, appeared unstoppable as he racked up 258 yards rushing and five touchdowns on 23 carries. This team, whom many people had written off earlier in the season, became Regional Champions by a convincing 35-14 score.

In spite of our victory, we certainly realized we didn't have time to be resting on our laurels. Later that evening, we found out we were going to be playing East Central in the semi-state game on their home field. This was the same team we had beaten at their place in overtime the year before, so we knew they would be looking for retribution. We also knew East Central had a tremendous team and, as luck would have it, they had nineteen returning starters. As I noted earlier, we were down to two returning starters from the previous season on offense — Mark Evans and Nick Marshall. Defensively, we only had Pat Kuntz, our big junior defensive end, and Tim Sergi as returning starters — and Tim was now only playing offense as our primary ball carrier. As such, one could argue that we only had three returning starters from the previous year. Now, we were facing nineteen East Central returning starters from the team we had barely beaten in overtime the previous year.

On paper, things didn't look good. However, the game isn't played on paper, it's played on a field and it is played from the heart. Height, weight and a person's year in school can all be measured and recorded on a roster. What you can't measure is the amount of heart a player competes with. Without question, the 2003 team played with an unbelievable amount of heart. They had a knack for making up for what they were lacking in size and speed. Against East Central, it would take everything they could muster.

Chris Strykowski, our special teams coach, spent a great deal of time working with Kevin Trulock, our senior place kicker. Chris had always done a phenomenal job with our kicking game and we knew this would be a vital part of the game. All three phases, offense, defense and the kicking game, were in high gear throughout the first half and we had a 10-0 lead at the end of the first quarter when Kevin nailed a 40-yard field goal. We had extended our lead to 16-3 at the half since our defense was able to keep their highly potent offense in check. However, we knew they were a veteran group, playing on their home turf in front of over 10,000 screaming fans and they would never surrender.

While we had clearly outplayed East Central in the first half, the reverse was true in the second. They played like a veteran team fighting for their lives. Midway through the fourth quarter, they brought the score to within 5 points (19-14.) Kevin

Trulock kicked a 38-yard field goal in the third quarter to get us to 19. Then, after a long Roncalli drive in the fourth, he kicked a 25-yard field goal for his third score that night. This gave us a 22-14 lead with about two minutes to go in the game. Despite the fact that our only scores in the second half were two field goals, our primary offensive weapon was our quarterback, Chris Schmaltz. He had a very strong arm, but started the season a little shaky. A big part of that slow start tied in with young and inexperienced linemen. However, by this point in the season, he was throwing like an All-American. His 191 yards passing in the game were what allowed us to put 22 points on the board against a stout East Central defense. I've often said we wouldn't have even been in the game if he hadn't played the game of his life. He certainly picked the right night to do it.

Leading 22-14 with about two minutes to play, the pressure was on our defense to make a huge stop. However, their quarterback had a great night as well and he led his team right down the field with pin-point passing. With only seconds left in regulation, he threw a perfect strike over the middle for the score. He also threaded the needle for the 2-point conversion, hitting his wide receiver on a quick slant right between two of our defenders.

Suddenly, we were facing a score tied at 22-22 at the end of regulation. This meant, for the second year in a row, in the same stadium against the same team (19 of their starters were the same kids), at the same end of the field, we were going into overtime. The consequences were clear-cut. The winners were going to play the following weekend for the State Championship, while the losers were going to be packing away their equipment on Monday suffering from a heartbreaking loss. We won the coin toss and elected to be on defense first. This meant East Central was going to have the ball first on the 10 yard line with four plays to score. They had certainly seized the momentum at the end of regulation and seemed very focused and confident when their offense took the field. Two plays later, their quarterback threw another perfect pass over the middle for the score and their PAT kick was perfect as well.

Our entire season rested on the shoulders of our offense and our opponents were holding a 29-22 lead. After three solid running plays, we faced a fourth down on their 2 yard line. Tim Sergi had played like a warrior and although he was battered and torn, he wanted the ball again regardless of the fact that it would place the weight of the entire season squarely on his shoulders. We ran him on a power toss left, he made a great cut behind his kickout blocker and plunged into the end zone. I was very tempted to go for two points and the win, but allowed the assistants to talk me out of it. So, we kicked the PAT instead. The kick was good for the tie, yet as the ball left Kevin's foot for the uprights, an opposing defensive end on a "hot rush" to try to block the kick slammed into our kicker's leg — bringing a flag for roughing the kicker.

Our immediate dilemma was: do we keep the point and the tie, which would send the game into a second overtime where we would have the ball first; or, do we take the penalty, remove the game-tying point from the scoreboard and have the ball moved to the 1 1/2 yard line where we could go for the two-point conversion and the win. Most people would probably tell you to never take points off the board, but my decision to go for two and the win was a simple one to make. First of all, the momentum was all in their favor and I really didn't want to go into another overtime. Secondly, and much more importantly, we run a power offense. I firmly believed if we couldn't gain at least 1 1/2 yards on any given play, we didn't deserve to win. Like we always do, we had pre-scripted our overtime and had rehearsed our 2-point play in the event that it became necessary. Finally, all of our players were confident with the game plan and wanted to go for the win.

We shifted our personnel up front a bit, sent a man in motion and ran Tim on a toss play to the left once again. For what seemed like an eternity, Tim cut up, slammed into the line of scrimmage and was stood up. Our offensive line continued to drive their feet as Tim twisted, turned and finally fell into the end zone. The line judge immediately shot his hands into the air to signal "TOUCHDOWN" and the Roncalli stands went wild. For the second time in three weeks, this team had accomplished the near impossible! On paper, this group had no business winning the semi-state championship, nor did many predict they would be going back to the RCA Dome for a second consecutive appearance in the 4A state finals. Thankfully this game isn't played on paper.

Our opponent in the State Championship game was an outstanding 13-1 team from East Noble. Their offense was fast and explosive, and their defense was quick and aggressive. However, if Chris Schmaltz and Kevin Trulock were the heroes of the East Central game the week before, Tim Sergi and our entire defensive squad were the standouts in the state game on the turf. Tim started by scoring in the first quarter with a 34-yard run. After a second quarter field goal, we took a 10-0 lead into the locker room at the half. It was more of the same in the second half. Tim had a 66-yard touchdown run with about three minutes left in the third quarter to give us a solid 17-0 lead. He finished the game with 208 rushing yards, just three yards shy of the 4A State Game record. Our defense, under coach Belch's guidance, turned in a phenomenal "bend but don't break" performance by shutting out the high octane East Noble offense. In Roncalli's seven State Championship games, no Roncalli defense had ever pitched a shutout. The fact that this group was the first to do so was a truly remarkable feat!

At the victory party at Roncalli after the game, I again addressed the crowd and thanked everyone for a truly wonderful season. Since this would have been Jonathan Page's senior year, I called Scott and Holly, his parents, up on the stage. This time, I presented my state medal to Holly. I was pleased that I could give them both medals to represent what would have been Jonathan's junior and senior seasons. I also wanted them to know that their family was still very much in our thoughts and prayers.

After each season, I put together a "football yearbook" for our players, including pictures, stats, game summaries and a letter I personally write to the team. The last two paragraphs of the letter I wrote to this team might best summarize my thoughts of this group:

> *Seniors, there is no question that you were the main ingredient in the development of this team. What you lacked in size and overall natural ability, you more than made up for with great leadership, positive attitudes, determination, and an outright will to win. I firmly believe we have an obligation to make the most of the gifts God has given us. This season, Seniors, you made the entire Roncalli family very proud as you proved to the entire state that you have what it takes to be Champions! Even more importantly, I believe you made God proud by using your gifts to the best of your ability. You became men in God's eyes and His are the ones that count!*
>
> *You will always be remembered as the team that proved what can happen when you combine work ethic, commitment and belief in yourselves with a strong faith in God. This is one of those "life lessons" I hope you will take with you for the rest of your lives. It will serve you well. Again, I wish you only the best always. I am very proud to say I was part of the 2003 State Championship Team! Thank you for allowing me to be a part of your lives. It has truly been an honor.*

The post-season letter in the team yearbook seemed like a very small tribute to such a wonderful group of young men — considering what they accomplished. That season, we had all endured a long and emotional roller coaster ride with many ups and downs, twists and turns. Ultimately, we were all better men because of it.

In the final analysis, I think they all know how much I love and respect them. That's what matters most.

The Roncalli Coaching Staff right after the 2003 State Championship Game.

First Row, L to R: Chris Strykowski, Chris Belch, Ray Shelburn, Bobby Griffin.
Back Row, L to R: Bruce Scifres, Jerre McManama, Eddie Keller, Brian Lauck, Tim Puntarelli

CHAPTER 12

Tradition vs. Recruiting

I must tell you the truth. Several years ago on Thanksgiving weekend, we were in the RCA Dome taking the field to begin pre-game warm ups for the State Championship game. When we ran past the opposing team's cheer block, they began shouting insults about us being cheaters — that our players had been recruited, etc. Normally, I don't pay any attention to the opposing team's fans, but this group was unusually loud and unruly. As I glanced up into the crowd, I could see a large number of them were wearing T-shirts that read "TRADITION VS. RECRUITING" in big, bold letters. This school had a fine football team. They were undefeated in thirteen games. Yet, when I saw that most of their fans were wearing these shirts, I became very confident that we would win the game. My confidence stemmed from the fact that they already had created a built-in excuse to lose. Although the match was close and came down to the last minute before the final score was decided, we made the crucial plays when we had to and ended up winning. As their fans filed out after the game, I'm certain cheating was the topic, and recruiting was the sin.

More recently, a team beat us in overtime in game eight of our regular season on our home field. Although we had over 400 yards of offense and our defense held them to just 200 yards, their special teams had played superbly and controlled field position throughout the game. The bottom line was that their kids made some huge plays in clutch situations. Consequently, I truly believe they deserved to win the game. Since they remained undefeated, their fans were ecstatic and stormed the field, and had a huge celebration in the middle of our game field. Although I was disappointed for our kids who had played their hearts out, I was proud of their kids for the way they had played — and I was happy for their fans as well. I knew if we could improve and somehow win our sectional, we would very likely see them again in the Regional game.

As luck would have it, we did meet them in a regional match-up on their home field. They were still undefeated and their team played admirably. The game went back and forth until late in the fourth quarter. Although we were trailing, we put together a scoring drive to take a four point lead with about a minute to play. Our defense was able to hold on and we pulled out a narrow victory. Both teams had played their hearts out; however, we made the big plays down the stretch and consequently, this time, we prevailed.

Unfortunately, as our players and fans were leaving the stadium, many of them were accosted by the opposing crowd. Our fans and players were being cursed at and accused of that same old recruiting and cheating bit. One silly woman was shouting, "We know you recruited your quarterback from Nebraska." Our quarterback was in the group being yelled at and he politely replied, "No ma'am, I have lived on the south side of Indianapolis all my life!" More accusations and insults were hurled at the group. Hearing all of this after the game, I couldn't help but wonder why their crowd had acted so differently five weeks earlier when their community was celebrating on our field. Nobody complained about cheating or recruiting then. As proud as I was of their community just five weeks earlier, I was equally disappointed in the way they dealt with this loss.

I firmly believe there is a fine line between being misinformed and mentally weak. Let me explain. If someone believes inaccurate information is true because that's all they've been exposed to, ignorance is understandable (though not enviable.) However, if that same person receives true information with evidence to prove it, yet continues to believe the false information, they cross the line from being misinformed to being mentally weak. Ignorance is understandable. Yet, most people have little tolerance for mental weakness. Personally, I've never heard a good excuse for someone with this malady.

Roncalli is a Catholic, parochial diocesan high school. Over the years, there have been five primary misconceptions about what this means, which I would like to address with factual information. Certainly one can continue to remain misinformed if they so choose. My hope is that clarifying the issue might result in a clear picture of what actually goes on. Mental strength is a choice as well.

> <u>Misconception #1</u>: **We recruit great athletes to come play for us.** This is absolutely false. We are a parochial school, not a private school, and there is a difference! As a parochial school, we have nine Catholic grade schools that feed into Roncalli. Each year, over 97% of our student population comes from these small Catholic grade schools. The remaining 3% DO NOT come to us because they were recruited. They come to Roncalli because their parents decide they want to pay tuition in order for their child to have a Catholic education. I have NEVER recruited a public school player for our team — and I never will. Over the years, critics from public schools have said, "Well, you have nine feeder schools to draw from, we only have our one middle school!" The point I always make in return is that our Catholic grade schools are relatively small. Our two largest are St. Barnabas and St. Jude, which normally have between thirty and thirty-five eighth grade boys each year. The two smallest are St. Rose and Central Catholic, which usually have fewer than ten eighth grade boys per year. As a result, each year, we have approximately 160 eighth grade males at our feeder schools, which is where nearly all of

our players come from. There are some Catholic schools that are not affiliated with the archdiocese. Consequently, they are considered private not diocesan. Since they don't have specific feeder schools, they can draw students from anywhere and some of these schools aggressively pursue good athletes to come to their school. Unfortunately, many people don't understand the difference between parochial and private, and therefore assume all Catholic schools can go out and recruit whomever they choose. This is simply not true.

I'd like to make another point along this same line. In 1984, a wonderful athlete named Danny Bauer played for Roncalli and was offered a full ride to play for Indiana University — where he ended up having a great collegiate career. Over the next twenty years, Roncalli didn't have one player who received an offer to play for a Big Ten caliber team. During my fifteen years at Roncalli, we have had six players who received Division I scholarships to Ball State, Toledo and Miami of Ohio — all members of the MAC Conference. It wasn't until twenty-one years later that we had another player who received a Big Ten caliber offer (which I'll cover more in the next chapter.) My point is this: In the past, I have jokingly said, "If we are out recruiting great players to come play for us, we must be doing a lousy job!" I have worked hard to educate people over the years on this subject and, by now, most fairly intelligent people know we don't recruit outside our nine small southside Catholic grade schools which feed into Roncalli.

<u>Misconception # 2</u>: **Our good athletes are on athletic scholarships.** This, too, is simply not true. Our players continue to laugh and joke about this because every one of them is paying several thousand dollars in tuition in order to attend our school. I repeat ... we do not have athletic scholarships. As far as I know, the only students who don't pay to go to Roncalli are the children of teachers in our

155

building who have been there for more than ten years. About three years ago, our school board passed a policy which gave teachers a 10% discount for each year they have taught at Roncalli. This is a great incentive to keep the "old timers" around. As far as I know, these are the only students who do not pay to go to our school.

<u>Misconception # 3:</u> **We have selective enrollment, where we pick and choose who we want in our school.** This is false. In short, any family willing to pay our tuition can send their child to Roncalli. No one, as yet, has been turned away. In Indiana, parents can send their children to any public school they want — provided they are willing to pay tuition. Interestingly, public school tuition is less than what our students are paying to come to Roncalli.

<u>Misconception # 4:</u> **All of our families are upper middle class.** Although some of our families are financially well-off, most are hard working, blue collar, middle class families. We also have some lower income families who make great sacrifices to send their kids to our school. Many of our parents even work a second job to afford the tuition. Obviously, they wouldn't make these kinds of sacrifices if they didn't feel it was worth it.

<u>Misconception # 5:</u> **We have no special needs students in our building who count as part of the enrollment numbers for the classification of sports.** This is absolutely false. Roncalli has just over 10% of its student population that qualifies for special needs status. This is not too far off the public school norm in Indiana.

These are the facts.

Recently, a public school coach asked me, "Okay. If you don't recruit, you don't have kids on scholarship, don't exercise selective enrollment and have some lower as well as upper income families, how do you explain all the success your school has in football?" There are three or four reasons I gave him for our success.

First of all, success breeds success. We have all heard this before and there's truth to it. Allow me to cite examples from some other sports. In Boy's Track, John Campbell led Gary Roosevelt to nine consecutive state titles in the 1980's. Soon after his retirement, their success in track began to decline. In Girl's Volleyball, under the direction of Steve Shondell, Muncie Burris has won eleven of the last thirteen State Championships. From 1987 through 2002 — a sixteen-year time span — Ben Davis, under the direction of Dick Dullaghan, won seven State Championships in 5A football. Fort Wayne Northrup has won the past six State Championships in girls track. Most impressively, under several different coaches, Carmel High School has won the last nineteen consecutive state titles in Girl's Swimming. All five of these are public schools, which have established outstanding winning traditions. Roncalli has won eight State Championships in football in the last twenty years — and four of these titles were earned within the last six years.

In the 2004 season, we became the first Indiana High School to win eight State Championships in football. In all fairness, should we be regarded any differently than Carmel, Gary Roosevelt, Muncie Burris, Ben Davis or Fort Wayne Northrup simply because we are a Catholic diocesan school? When you combine success with a program that teaches hard work, fundamentals, discipline and other "Lifetime Lessons," you've laid the foundation for tradition. Our southside Catholic grade school players dream of the day they will wear a Roncalli jersey — hoping to grab their own piece of the legacy. Our CYO grade school program, with long-time director, Ed Tinder, has a lot to do with this.

After our 1999 State Championship, Bill Benner, a sportswriter for the Indianapolis Star wrote:

Southside Catholic football is a tradition passed from generation to generation, from family to family, from father to son, from parish to parish and from neighbor-hood to neighborhood. At the grade school level, in CYO competition on Saturday mornings, tough little knotheads wear oversized pads and helmets, and endeavor to knock the living daylights out of one another. It's their first taste of what it means to be keepers of the flame that burns so brightly, to learn lessons of legacy and to realize the direct correlation between hard work and success. Then, at the high school level, they set aside differences, animosities and rivalries. They are no longer playing for Saint Some-one. They now play for Roncalli, and Roncalli football is more than high school football. It's tradition, a treasure and a way of life.

No better summation of the Roncalli tradition and legacy has ever been written. In my opinion, if we do have an "unfair advantage" as a Catholic school, it is that we are a Christ-centered institution that has no restrictions on prayer or our ability to teach the same lessons Jesus taught about God's love for each of us. I will always believe creating a concept of family between coaches and players and the larger community as a whole establishes a very powerful bond. The mission of our school only serves to strengthen this bond.

Finally, I believe the most important reason we win more than "our fair share" of games is that every high school player in the country wants to play hard to make his parents and loved ones proud. Every teenage boy wants to get his name on the loudspeaker and in the newspaper on Saturday morning, and to be noticed by his peers, both male and female. Every athlete wants to be recognized in their school community for doing something positive with his abilities. Our players want all of these things as well. However, if there is one thing I do well as a coach, I have been able to convince our kids that it's their duty and obligation to make the most of the countless gifts God has given them. Our kids play with a sense of purpose that's un-common among high school aged athletes. Their personal resolve far exceeds simply playing for themselves, their parents, their girlfriend or their coaches.

They play like men to make all of these people proud, but they also play so intensely because they see it as their obligation to make good on their promise to use the gifts they've had bestowed upon them. It is also founded in the concept that you should do your best to bring glory and honor to His name by the way you conduct yourself and live your life — both on and off the field. If we have an "unfair advantage" at Roncalli, it could be a result of having the ability to talk about these things with our players on a daily basis. Quite frankly, I feel sorry for the coaches around the country who are not permitted to do so.

Remember, I believe there is a distinction between being misinformed and mentally weak. Those who continue to echo the criticisms about recruiting and cheating continue in fact to give themselves a built-in excuse for why they aren't successful. If coaches and communities pass that on to their players, it serves as a disadvantage; weak excuses only decrease a team's odds of winning a big game. Even though I may be doing a disservice to our own program, I think it's more important that I continue to try to educate the misinformed. Wise folks could use this knowledge to make themselves stronger, and ultimately that could be detrimental to us.

There you have it; everyone deserves the opportunity to be educated. That's the truth. No lie.

CHAPTER 13

Team of Destiny

Some things are just meant to be. Coming off consecutive State Championship seasons in 2002 and 2003, the prospects for the 2004 season seemed very bright indeed. We were returning the majority of our starters and our upcoming senior class boasted perhaps the best physical talent the school had ever seen. Three players in particular were being heavily recruited by Big Ten schools. Tim Sergi, our running back who had rushed for 2,500 yards as a junior; Pat Kuntz, our 6' 4", 250-lb. defensive end, and Jason Werner, our 6' 5" free safety who had placed fourth in the 200-meter dash the previous spring in the state track meet were all getting a lot of attention. Our other returning starters were outstanding as well since we had fifteen of the twenty-two starting positions returning.

In addition to being very gifted athletes, our seniors were very strong academically, had great work ethics and were extremely focused. Saying expectations were high for this group would be a huge understatement. Knowing these guys were also fun-loving and each had a great sense of humor only added to the excitement and anticipation the coaching staff had as the start of the season approached.

Moreover, our 2004 seniors had the potential to be great leaders. At the end of two-a-day's, the players voted for captains and the results were interesting. In years past, we typically had three or four players who would clearly receive more votes than anyone else and they would become our captains. For the first time ever, eight players received a substantial number of votes — without much separation. I felt this was a good indication of the great senior leadership we had received in the off-season. Therefore, we decided to have four offensive and four defensive captains. Leading our offense was Tim Sergi, Andrew Hasty (quarterback), Taylor Donnell (tight end) and Zac Kidwell (fullback.) Our defensive captains were: Pat Kuntz, Jason Werner, Brad Stephenson (outside linebacker) and Chad Peterman (cornerback.) Although we had never done this before, I was convinced these eight players would do a great job leading our team in quest of our third consecutive title.

In our much anticipated season opener at Center Grove, our offense moved the ball effectively. These efforts were led by Tim Sergi, who had two touchdown runs, and Andrew Hasty with two long passes to Jason Werner — one of which resulted in a score. Jason was playing with a good-sized cast on his arm since he had broken his wrist right before the start of the season. Chris Belch and Brian Lauck had prepared our defense and our secondary superbly and we shut out Center Grove's highly explosive Wing-T attack. Billy Cobb, our inside linebacker and the leading tackler during the previous season, registered twelve tackles. Our secondary also pulled down three interceptions to shut down their passing game. Center Grove scored a safety after an errant Roncalli punt snap, however, which made the final margin 24-2. After losing our opening game during the previous two seasons, we were off to a great start!

Our second game in the 2004 season, which was at Franklin Central, was just as highly anticipated. This was Franklin Central's first home game in their new stadium which had been built in the off-season and was beautiful. By game time there was still a very long line outside the gates waiting to get tickets. Since the stadium was already packed, Brian Avery (my brother-in-law and Franklin Central's Athletic Director) was forced to turn people away. The atmosphere was electrifying. Both teams played hard-nosed defense, but Tim Sergi's long touchdown run and Andrew Hasty's long touchdown pass to Chad Peterman led us to a narrow 13-6 victory.

Game #3 proved to be equally as tough, as it was at home against Chatard — the defending 3A State Champion. In pre-season polling, two of the top candidates for the Mr. Football Award, an honor given to the best football player in the state, were the featured ball carriers for each team. In fact, Tim Sergi, who had enjoyed a "monster" season as a junior, and Dray Mason, the highly talented ball carrier from Chatard, were probably the front-runners for this esteemed award. As fate would have it, Dray suffered a high ankle sprain early in the first quarter. Since this type of injury takes several weeks to heal, he ended up missing most of the regular season during his senior year. Even in his absence, the game was very close. Tim Curren, our place kicker, converted a field goal with just a couple of minutes left to lead us to a 10-7 victory. This made our record 3-0 against some of the better football programs in the state and we were looking forward to the remainder of our regular season.

In game four, we had to travel north to play South Bend St. Joe, a Catholic high school across the street from the University of Notre Dame. Through most of the first quarter, Tim averaged eight or nine yards a carry. From every indication, this was going to be a big night for him. In fact, with Dray Mason out for several weeks, the game could be a big step in his quest for the Mr. Football award. After a 10-yard gain towards the end of the first quarter, Tim took a blow to his knee from the side. He got up slowly and walked gingerly toward our sideline. Mike Sahm, our outside linebacker coach and a certified athletic trainer, and Jeff Peterson, our outstanding team doctor, immediately put Tim through a thorough sideline medical exam. Before long, Tim was up and running on the sideline, looking crisp with his cuts and strong as ever. He is one of the most competitive young men I have ever known, which is a key factor in his prowess as a running back. Soon, he was pleading to get back on the field. As a senior co-captain and one of our hardest workers, he was more than deserving.

After returning to the game, he broke loose on a 15-yard gain around the left end. As he approached a defensive back, he cut hard on his right leg to try to break to the sideline but his knee gave out and he went down without ever being hit. For a short time, he lay on the field and was then assisted to the sideline. We had several other backs rotate in and went on to win the game 35-0. However, our victory came at a huge cost. The following day, we received the crushing news that Tim had torn his ACL and would most likely miss the rest of the season.

Tim's injury was heartbreaking because he only needed 1,600 yards rushing to break our all-time career rushing record. Since he had rushed for over 2,500 yards during his junior year and had almost his entire line back, becoming our school's all-time leading rusher appeared to be a foregone conclusion. The fact that he had been the front-runner for the Mr. Football Award only added to the disappointment. Most of all, I was heartsick for Tim and his family. Frank and I were coaching together when Tim was born and I had grown to respect and admire the entire Sergi family. If someone were to ask me to write a book on how any coach would want parents to conduct themselves, Frank and Trish would be my models! Tim's great attitude, work ethic and warrior mentality had always made him deserving of the success he had achieved. Watching what the family had to go through for the remainder of the season was heartbreaking.

Ironically, the St. Joe game essentially marked the end of Tim's season, however, it also marked a new beginning for Nate Ashworth. After sitting out the previous year, Nate had worked extremely hard — both mentally and physically — to return to school full-time and to rejoin the football team as a "fifth year" senior. By that time, he had regained about fifty percent of the use of his right arm and right leg, and hadn't missed a practice since the start of two-a-days. This young man who had undergone a stroke eighteen months before was an incredible inspiration to our entire school community. His unbelievable attitude, gentlemanly demeanor and the constant smile on his face won him the respect and admiration of every person in our building. Late in the third quarter, after Tim had already left the stadium, Nate went in for a few plays on the defensive line. After playing with a great deal of courage and determination, we brought him back out. As he ran back to our sideline, players, coaches and all of our fans gave him a long and well-deserved standing ovation.

Like Tim, I can remember coaching with Nate's father, Bob, when he was born. Eighteen years earlier, I had no idea I would be coaching both of them, along with Andrew Hasty, on the same team. I also had no idea that I would have to watch both the Ashworth and Sergi families struggle through the life changing injuries to their sons. However, I was fully aware of the character and integrity both families possessed. These traits would prove vital to helping their sons endure the burden of heartbreak and disappointment. On that September night up in South Bend, I felt blessed to have been able to play a role in the development of each of these young men's lives.

At that point, we were facing the remainder of the season without one of the best running backs to ever wear a Roncalli uniform and our most immediate concern was who would become the starting tailback — in a tailback oriented offense — for our upcoming game against Scecina? At various times during the first four games, Kirk Cahill, a sophomore with a running style that was very similar to Tim's, had filled in admirably. Chris Merkel, a stocky, hard running junior, had also gotten some reps and did a fine job. Perhaps the most intriguing player was Scott Lutgring, a senior who had started the St. Joe game at the flanker/slotback position. Lutty, as he was called by his teammates, was 5' 9" and around 170 lbs. Since he had an impeccable work ethic in the weight room, he was a solid ball of muscle.

Over the years, we've had several players come through our program who have had more natural ability than Lutty. However, we have never had anyone who worked harder, was more focused and determined, or who was more driven than this young man. Even though he wasn't a starter through the end of two-a-days, he was always at the front of the pack during drills and conditioning. It was obvious he wasn't going to let anyone outwork him. Every great running back I have ever coached has had the same burning desire — the competitive edge that would never allow them to surrender. Without question, this was Lutty's strongest trait. As a result, and because he was a senior, we decided to allow him to start at tailback against Scecina — even though he didn't have much experience in that position. He rushed for over 150 yards in a decisive Roncalli victory. We were not disappointed.

We were now 5-0 and our sixth game was against a very talented Cathedral team. We knew their 1-4 record was quite deceptive since their first two losses were to Ben Davis and Warren Central — the top two 5A programs in Indiana. Despite the fact they lost those games, they put up a fight and played very tough. They lost their next two games to Cincinnati St. X, one of Ohio's top programs, and Chatard. They came close to winning both games but gave up scores in the last couple of minutes to lose by narrow margins. They won their fifth game in decisive fashion and were primed and ready to take us on at their home field. Just as one might expect, many people were misled by the records of the two teams and assumed we would win quite easily. After watching film, it was obvious to our staff that this was going to be one of the toughest opponents we played all year.

In a seesaw battle, we had to come from behind to tie the score at 17-17 with about three minutes to play. Cathedral answered by putting together a long drive and made masterful use of time by kicking a field goal with about three seconds on the clock. In the end, they beat us 20-17. Our dream of an undefeated season was gone. Yet, of greater concern was the fact that Cathedral was in our sectional. With Tim Sergi out and Jason Werner still in an arm cast, there was still a lot of work to do.

We managed to regroup somewhat and win game seven 45-7. However, game eight was our homecoming against a very good, undefeated Mooresville team. Lutty played the game of his life as he rushed for 280 yards and caught passes for another 70 yards. His offensive total of 350 yards set a new single game record at Roncalli. Our offense more than doubled their total yardage, but the Mooresville's kicking game continued to put us deep in our own territory to start each drive. Their players made several huge plays in the second half and took a 28-21 lead with about five minutes to play. We came back to drive the length of the field and punched in a score with about thirty seconds to go. My immediate inclination was to go for two since we had over 400 yards of total offense. Plus, I felt we had momentum on our side. However, all but one of our assistants thought we should kick the PAT to send it into overtime. I decided to go with the sentiment of the staff, so we kicked the PAT to send the game into overtime. We had the ball first, got to the 2 yard line in three plays and kicked a field goal to take a 31-28 lead. Three plays later, they completed a pass over the middle for a score and won our homecoming game 34-31 in overtime. After seeming invincible in the first half of the season, and for the second time in three weeks, the mighty Rebels had fallen.

After practice the following Monday, I gathered all the seniors together. I was very frank and told them I had some concerns about the chemistry of the team. I observed that there were some egos which were standing in the way of us becoming a great team. I told them until they put these divisive attitudes aside, we would never accomplish our goal of making Indiana high school football history. Then, I left the thrity-one seniors on the field to have a meeting and discuss what needed to be done to make the team better. I let them know that I wanted each senior to take the opportunity to speak his mind. As I walked away, I expected the meeting to last thirty to forty minutes. In fact, they didn't come off the field until almost two and a half hours later.

At practice the next day, all of the seniors had a sense of urgency and enthusiasm that had been lacking in recent weeks. Looking back, I'm convinced the long senior meeting was the turning point that season. They seemed to have a newfound resolve not to lose another game during their time together as a team. Their enthusiasm paid off and we beat our next three opponents by a combined score of 109-31.

Our sectional championship game was against our old nemesis, Cathedral, on their home field — once again, where they had dashed our hopes of an undefeated season just six weeks earlier. To make matters worse, Pat Kuntz, our all-state defensive end and starting left offensive tackle, had broken his right arm in the previous week's game. He had a large cast that extended above his elbow, which kept his arm bent at a 90 degree angle. The doctor gave permission for him to play — as much as pain and a casted, bent arm would allow. At best, we were hoping to get a few defensive plays out of him, but knew we would have to reconfigure our offensive line.

Casey Bolsega was our right tackle and had been having a great season (and ended up being named to the All-State Team.) We decided to move Andy Hillstrom, our 5' 10", 220-lb. right guard, to left tackle in Pat's place. Even though he was a two year starter and a fine lineman, he was outsized by Cathedral's defensive ends who were 6' 5", 265 lbs. and 6' 3", 250 lbs. respectively. Furthermore, Sean McMahon, Andy's backup at guard, was under 200 lbs. We knew this would be a very physical game. Without the services of Tim Sergi and Pat Kuntz, two of the best players we have had in my time at Roncalli, our prospects for victory seemed a little bleak. Nevertheless, after everything these seniors had been through over the previous three seasons, we knew they would never surrender.

In typical Roncalli-Cathedral fashion, the game was a true slug-fest filled with hard-hitting and emotional play. Midway through the first quarter, we drew first blood when Lutty broke loose for a 56-yard touchdown run but missed the PAT. On their next possession, Cathedral marched down the field and took the lead at 7-6. At the end of the first quarter, Tim Curren nailed a 22-yard field goal to put us in front; 9-7. In the second quarter, Cathedral put together a scoring drive to take a 13-9 lead. However, we stopped their 2-point conversion attempt to keep us trailing by only four points at the half.

Although neither team moved the ball very well in the second half, Cathedral kicked a 19-yard field goal towards the end of the third quarter and took a 16-9 lead. With 8:42 remaining, Matt Heskett, one of our cornerbacks, intercepted an errant pass and returned it to midfield. The ensuing drive was pressure-packed. On third and five, Andrew Hasty made a great fake on a misdirection play, concealed the ball nicely and ran the opposite way for an 11-yard gain and a big first down. As the clock wound down, we were facing a third and nine from the Cathedral 35 yard line. Andrew threw a perfect 24-yard completion to Lutty out of the backfield to the eleven yard line. With about three minutes on the clock, I opened my trusty red binder and turned to the overtime script. Even though we weren't in overtime, we were trailing by seven and the balance of the season was resting on our ability to punch in a score. The script served us well and we picked up nine yards in three plays to make it fourth and one from the 2 yard line.

Interestingly enough, two nights before I had awakened during the night because of a dream that we were at the goal line facing a fourth and one as time was expiring. Since Cathedral was so big and physical, and Pat Kuntz wasn't in our offensive lineup, plowing them out of the way didn't seem like a feasible option. It was at that time (about 2:00 A.M.) that the concept to have Jason Werner, our free safety, line up at tailback to have him jump over the pile came to me. At 6' 5", Jason was one of the fastest and most athletic players I have ever coached, and was the best leaper on the team. The next evening at practice, we installed "Jason Over the Top." After practicing the play a few times, I informed the team we would use this play if we needed a yard to win the game. Ironically, this was exactly the position we found ourselves in. Behind wedge blocking up front, Jason leaped high in the air — almost doing a complete flip — and crossed the goal line to bring us within 1 point.

I hadn't forgiven myself for our loss to Mooresville when I hadn't trusted my instincts and allowed myself to be talked out of going for two. This time there wasn't going to be a discussion. For a couple of weeks, we had been working on a play in which we would shift to an unbalanced set, line Jason up at quarterback in the shotgun, motion a back across the formation, then sprint Jason away from the loaded side to the corner of the end zone. As we had anticipated, Cathedral adjusted to our shift. When the ball was snapped, I thought Jason would go untouched into the end zone. To my horror, their linebacker shot underneath our tackle, who was supposed to chip off and pick him up, and came flying across, untouched, and slammed into Jason at full speed. In one of the finest plays I have ever seen in a high school game, Jason miraculously balanced himself on one hand as his legs were knifed out from under him, regained his balance and footing, and drove into the corner of the end zone. As our stands erupted into a deafening roar, it was nothing short of pandemonium on the sidelines and on our bench. But, the game wasn't over yet. Cathedral staged one last drive but, with thirty-six seconds left on the clock, Jason secured his second interception of the game to lead us to a 17-16 victory. We had avenged our loss from earlier in the season and managed to accomplish it without two of our best players!

Our sectional championship set up a regional match against Mooresville, who had beaten us earlier in the season and was still undefeated. The game was on their home field and we knew there was going to be a huge crowd. With Pat Kuntz's broken arm still on the mend, we had to continue with the same "shuffled" lineup we had the week before. In game planning, we focused on bolstering our kicking game, which is where they had beaten us a few weeks earlier.

From the opening kickoff, the stadium was filled with electricity. We put together a sustained drive — mostly on the legs of Scott Lutgring, who ultimately punched it in from the 1 yard line for a 7-0 lead. Mooresville's first score came midway through the first quarter when we were deep in our own territory and a punt snap sailed over our punter's head for a safety. Before the end of the first quarter, Mooresville put together a scoring drive to take a 9-7 lead, which they carried into halftime.

Hasty threw the ball extremely well in the second half and hit Werner and Taylor Donnell, our big tight end, with some clutch passes. Toward the end of the third quarter, Lutty scored on a 7-yard run and we took a 13-9 lead. With five minutes to go in the fourth quarter, they had the ball and were facing a fourth and eleven from our 35 yard line. Catching us off guard, they perfectly executed an end around reverse pass for a score, which gave them a 16-13 lead. For the second week in a row, we were trailing and had to travel the length of the field in the last five minutes of the game.

Behind Lutty's determined running and Andrew's pinpoint passing we moved the ball up-field. The two key plays were Hasty's 30-yard pass over the middle to Donnell and, on third and twelve with 1:07 left in the game, he then hit Lutty on a 38-yard pass up the sideline to the one yard line. He finished the game with a very efficient eight for ten and 185 yards passing. After two quarterback sneaks were stopped, Jason was once again inserted for the "Jason Over the Top" play, which was successful. In a repeat of the previous week, Jason hauled in the game winning interception in the last few seconds of the game. He finished the night with three pass receptions for 90 yards, to go along with his school record four interceptions! He was quickly making a name for himself as one of the best playmakers in the state. Furthermore, for the second week in a row, he helped lead us to come-from-behind victories over two teams that had beaten us in the regular season.

The next week, we played our semi-state game at Roncalli

against an undefeated and highly talented Columbus East team. Indiana tournament weather was back in full swing and the playing conditions were damp and muddy. Columbus East put together a nice drive to score midway through the first quarter but Jason came flying off the edge to block the PAT to make the score 6-0. In the second quarter, we scored a safety after a bad punt snap. Then, right before the half, we took a 9-6 lead on a one-yard Lutgring run.

Throughout most of the third quarter, our teams went back and forth until their tailback broke loose for a 29-yard touchdown run. Then, they completed a pass for a 2-point conversion and took a 14-9 lead at the end of the third quarter. With less than five minutes remaining in the game and Columbus East at midfield with the ball, and the lead, they completed a pass over the middle. As the receiver turned up field Brad Stephenson, one of our co-captains, smashed into him jarring the ball loose. We recovered the ball at midfield, creating another come-from-behind possibility.

For the third week in a row, we were trailing in the last minutes of the game, fighting to put a score on the board to keep our playoff dreams alive. Lutty had been our workhorse throughout the game. In the second half, there were at least six times when he carried two or more defenders — along with our playoff dreams — on his back to just barely make the first down. In all my years of coaching, I can't remember a runner his size who was so hard to bring down. All of his hard work and dedication paid off. He rushed for 161 yards on 32 carries and definitely kept us in position to win the game. Taylor Donnell also made a huge 26-yard catch in the last drive. He literally took the ball away from the defender who had appeared to intercept the pass. With just under a minute remaining, Andrew was able to sneak it in which gave us a 15-14 lead. Columbus marched the ball out to midfield and, for the third week in a row, Jason intercepted a pass in the remaining seconds and secured the win for Roncalli.

In all my years of coaching, I've never seen a team have to come from behind in the last three minutes of the game, in three consecutive weeks and then have the same player intercept passes in the final seconds to end the game. When we were out at midfield celebrating our win over this outstanding team, it occurred to me that we would be returning to the State Championship game for a third consecutive year. It was at this time that I began to wonder if this team was, in fact, a "team of destiny."

Game preparation for state finals week is exciting. Whenever possible, we travel around that week to practice on artificial turf — since the RCA Dome has a turf field. As I have mentioned before, my favorite practice of the year is our Thanksgiving Day practice. It's a sharp, tune-up practice held at an indoor soccer facility. We always end the practice by allowing our players to share the things they are most thankful for with their "brothers" during the team prayer. I think this helps all of us keep the week in perspective.

Wawasee, our upcoming opponent, was 13-1 and had a tremendous team. Their running back was the state's leading rusher and their quarterback had passed for almost 2,000 yards and was an excellent ball carrier as well. We knew their offense was explosive since they had beaten their semi-state opponent 49-19 the previous week. Likewise, their defense was exceptionally fast and physical.

They opened the game with a "bloop kick" to our 35 yard line, which we bobbled and they recovered. As a result, we felt fortunate to hold them to just a field goal on their opening drive. On our ensuing possession, Lutty was picking up sizable gains as we marched down the field, however, a holding call deep in their territory stalled the drive. Wawasee answered with a long drive of their own and their quarterback scrambled in for a 13-yard touchdown with about eight minutes to go in the second quarter. This gave them a 10-0 lead. This quieted our crowd, but in truth, I don't think our kids batted an eye.

Brandon Axum returned the ensuing kickoff 48 yards to

our 49 yard line. Lining Jason up at flanker, we motioned him across in speed motion and he picked up 5 yards on a Jet Sweep. The next play, Jason motioned across again but we faked the sweep and handed off underneath to Zac Kidwell, our fullback, who rumbled 34 yards for the score. In our "I" backfield, our fullback is primarily a battering ram and absolutely must possess the heart of a warrior. Zac fit this description perfectly. It was extremely gratifying to watch him cross the goal line for our first score in the State Championship game. On Wawasee's next possession, Jason came up with a huge interception — his ninth during the tournament — to give us the ball with about four minutes in the half. Three plays later, Andrew hit Jason on a post pattern for a 46-yard score and a 14-10 lead at halftime.

We carried this momentum into the second half as Billy Perry, one of our inside linebackers, snagged an interception over the middle. Three plays later, Andrew hit Zac right up the middle on a seam route for a 30-yard touchdown — extending the lead to 21-10.

Earlier, I mentioned Tim Puntarelli. Tim is one of my best friends and our quarterback coach. As players, I was a running back and he was a quarterback. Therein lies our differences in offensive philosophies. Over the years, we have had some good natured teasing about his desire to put the ball in the air more often. These discussions have made us both better coaches. He has taught me to better appreciate the nuances of the passing game, which is against my nature. Likewise, he has grown to appreciate the "chess match" of blocking schemes and the diligence necessary to account for all defenders on every play. We usually average eight or nine passes per game but, as our quarterback coach, he would like to see more. His wish came true in the State Game.

After our opening drive, it became evident that Wawasee was determined to slow down our running game in general and our toss series in particular. In stacking their defense, other running plays became more effective. More importantly, they were forced to defend our wide receiver man-to-man. Andrew threw perfect strikes on post patterns to Jason and Chad Peterman in the third quarter, one which set up a one yard quarterback sneak — extending our lead to 28-10. Coach Belch and our defensive coaches had pieced together a wonderful game plan that kept both their running back and quarterback in check after their first two possessions. Along with excellent special teams play, our offense received good field position throughout most of the game.

The third quarter was the turning point in this game. As we took control of the contest, two rather inspiring events took place. Tim Sergi worked relentlessly after his knee surgery to try to make it back. We allowed him to dress for the Semi-State game the week before so he could run out of the woods (a pre-game ritual before home games) but he didn't enter the game. It was only fitting that he should get to play in the State Championship Game of his senior year. He wasn't really supposed to have contact, so we put him in at wide receiver for a few plays. He had worked so hard and kept such a positive attitude throughout his ordeal. Just like Nate's entry into the game at South Bend, it was a true testimony to the human spirit obtaining victory over adversity and disappointment. Tim was right where he belonged — in a Roncalli football uniform on the turf of the RCA Dome on Thanksgiving weekend. I do believe this was part of his destiny as a football player.

The second event occurred with about 2:30 remaining in the third quarter. With a 28-10 lead, our offense had stalled on their 28 yard line. Facing fourth down and beyond field goal range, I called timeout. We had been running a lot of speed motion across the formation to create trips to the strong side. So, the thought occurred to me to throw a corner route to the opposite side of the end zone to our flanker — the inside receiver on the trips side. When I jogged onto the field to give this play to the huddle, I was overcome by the warm, tingling sensation I had experienced so frequently over the last three seasons.

Phil Andrews, Karl's son, was a senior wide receiver who had never lined up in the flanker position. He had caught a few passes during the season but had never scored in a varsity game. It became apparent to me who my "visit" was from when I crossed the field to the huddle. So, I switched Phil to flanker and called the play.

Once again, we motioned to the trips and, as Andrew dropped back, he did an excellent job of "looking off" to the trips side, forcing the secondary to rotate. At the last second, he threw a beautiful pass to the opposite corner of the end zone, hitting Phil in stride for the score. Phil was immediately mobbed by his teammates. As he left the field with a huge smile on his face, I grabbed him in a big bear hug and whispered in his ear, "Phil, you know your dad was out there with you. Don't you?" He replied, "Yes, Coach. I know he was." Then, I added, "And, you know that he's very proud of you right now. Don't you?" He answered, "Thanks, Coach! I know that too!" As I looked in his eyes, I could see an immense amount of pride. He had been through so much and had grown into such a fine young man. His strength and mental toughness kept him from showing much emotion. I had to turn quickly away from him so he wouldn't see the tear tracing down my cheek. At that moment, I didn't possess either of those qualities.

Our defense stood strong through the fourth quarter. Pat Kuntz still had a large cast on his arm but it had been cut below his elbow, and it allowed him to play full-time on defense in the championship game. He played with a great deal of passion as he registered ten tackles and broke our career sack record. Billy Cobb, our middle linebacker, also had ten tackles and finished as our leading tackler for the second year in a row.

The only disappointment of the night occurred early in the fourth quarter as Lutty broke loose on an exciting 70-yard touchdown run, following a great downfield block by Andrew Hasty. Unfortunately, the line judge on our side threw a flag which called Lutty's touchdown back. This is the only time in the entire book when I have criticized an official and I am usually very careful <u>not</u> to do that. However, film verified that it was an awful call and one that kept Lutty from scoring in the championship game. With the heart that Lutty had played with all year, he deserved that score. Maybe it was destiny. Phil Andrews was the last player to score in the 2004 season and led us to a 35-10 victory.

My elation at winning the 2004 State Football Championship came after a season of hard work and determination on the part of the entire Roncalli coaching staff and all the players. These efforts culminated in the week leading up to the final game. That Monday, the sports editor for the Indianapolis Star called to ask if a sportswriter and a cameraman could meet me at the school on the morning of the state game. He wanted them to shadow me for the entire day and write an article on what game day is like from a coach's perspective. He assured me they would not be intrusive. My initial inclination was to decline. I told him I would probably not be good company in this setting. After his continued assurances, I finally agreed. Along with some wonderful pictures, a full two-page article was included in the Tuesday, November 30, 2004 edition. It was entitled "In the End, All Was Good." The following is the full article:

> *Finally, Bruce Scifres put down his playbook.*
>
> *It's a tattered red binder, filled with a decade and a half worth of handwritten plays.*
>
> *Scifres held the playbook tightly throughout the day Saturday, from the time the veteran Roncalli football coach arrived at school early in the morning until the moment the Rebels returned to the school from the RCA Dome nearly twelve hours later, state champions for the third year in a row.*
>
> *Upon their return, Scifres and his players entered the school through a door that led to a stage with the curtains closed. When the curtains opened, players stood before a gymnasium packed from floor to rafters with fans*

clad in red, white and blue, the school colors.

After delivering a quick speech, shaking hundreds of hands and receiving dozens of congratulatory hugs, Scifres stood alone, his arms crossed, with a look of satisfaction betrayed by a rare smile.

It was a different look from the man who spent most of his day stoic, focused on improving his record at the RCA Dome to 6-0.

Scifres awoke at 6:00 A.M., thinking of the best way for his linemen to block for the team's trademark power-toss run.

The forty-seven-year-old former high school and college running back and Roncalli coach for fifteen years had stayed up late the night before, secluded in his home office. His wife, Jackie, and the couple's children — Luke, thirteen; Abby, eleven; Cal, nine; and Meggie, seven — knew that Friday night would be a long "work night" after a day Scifres had spent with his team practicing at the dome.

Scifres set his playbook down about 1:00 A.M. to go to bed. When he arrived at school Saturday morning, Scifres would find a card inside, slipped in by Jackie. The envelope read, "To the coach."

"She always tries to remind me to enjoy the journey," Scifres said. "Sometimes I forget to do that."

MORNING RUSH

Scifres arrived at the school cafeteria early Saturday.

He directed student volunteers and sophomore football players on what footballs to take to the game and how many coolers of sports drinks to load.

He calmly answered a student's question about where to put the cookies.

"I enjoy just the coaching aspect a lot better than the other little logistical things that go into preparation,"

Scifres said. "It's more fun being an assistant coach.

"Anytime something goes wrong or something is forgotten or left behind, it's ultimately the head coach's responsibility. Those are things that can add to the stress of game day, too."

Scifres' quiet, focused manner is adopted by his players and revered by his peers.

"We can't tell you the value of having one-third of the male student population with him and the coaching staff for four months," athletic director Dave Toner said.

PRACTICE TIME

At 9:45 A.M., Scifres left the cafeteria for the Blockhouse, a plain separate building just north of the high school, which houses a locker room for players and coaches.

Inside, players had begun to arrive. Several lounged on worn couches and chairs, nodding to the beat of the music playing in the background.

Scifres moved quickly to the coaches' office, a simple room with a cluttered desk and long table with a few chairs placed around it. The room offered a glimpse of who Scifres is as a person: No frills. Basic. What you see is what you get.

There is no computer. An unframed pencil drawing of famed football coach Vince Lombardi on a plain white sheet of paper, hangs above the door.

Scifres was dressed in his game-day attire, navy blue cap, navy windbreaker, khaki pants and worn white tennis shoes. His only excess was the state-championship ring the Rebels won last year.

"I typically wear the most recent one," Scifres said.

Scifres was greeted by longtime assistant Tim Puntarelli, who showed Scifres some offensive plays he drew up on a sheet of paper.

"These are the pass plays," Puntarelli said with a smirk. "We won't use these anyway."

At 10:00 A.M., Scifres moved his players to the cafeteria to walk through different parts of the game plan.

The players who didn't participate in the walk-through stood in silent observation, with one occasionally getting the call to go in for a play.

Players had to be ready at all times. Scifres spoke a language players had to grasp quickly.

"All X's, Z-bubble is automatically a crack call," Scifres emphasized to his linemen, who nodded in comprehension.

Scifres would occasionally quiz players on where they needed to be in certain formations. He also invited questions.

When lineman Pat Kuntz needed clarification on a play, Scifres calmly coached the player and then asked, "Are you comfortable with all that stuff?"

Scifres took his team through game situations, presenting options for overtime and fourth-down situations.

As the walk-through wound down, Scifres gathered his players in close for a final talk before they reconvened at the dome.

"There will be a series when (Wawasee) stuffs us," he said. "Stay with it. I guarantee you, they have never played a team as relentless on offense as we're going to be."

SURPRISE STRATEGY

Scifres has adhered to few traditions on the morning of the state finals. He doesn't require the same breakfast — Saturday he had pancakes, though Jackie said he was too nervous to eat — or make the same pregame speech.

But one tradition that has held true is an 11:00 A.M. pregame Mass, said by the Rev. John McCaslin in the Blockhouse.

Scifres and his coaches then retired to their office.

Scifres conferred with his coaches about exploiting Wawasee's expected man coverage by passing the ball more.

Scifres was receptive to the idea, as he often is when seeking input from assistants.

"Most of them played for us at Roncalli," Scifres said of his coaches. "I put a lot of stock in their opinions and suggestions."

Scifres and his players returned to the cafeteria for a parent-provided lunch of pasta, breadsticks, salad, fruit and cookies.

TO THE DOME

At 1:30, Scifres boarded the lead bus in a convoy that left the school and headed toward the dome with an escort of five police cars. Sirens blared as traffic was halted.

Scifres was silent on the bus, and the players reflected their coach's demeanor.

Once inside the dome, Scifres and his players walked through the inner corridors to the visiting locker room. Inside, some players turned on a television to watch the Class 3A championship game. Others listened to music on their headphones.

Scifres retired to a small room for a few minutes of reflection.

"I pray a lot," Scifres said. "Any time I have to myself, I try to pray."

After the team took the field for warm-ups, Scifres sought out Wawasee coach Joe Rietveld and offered praise for the way the Warriors had played during the season.

He followed that with a cordial meeting with the game officials and ended it by saying he hoped the players were at the point in the season where there wouldn't be many mistakes — coach-speak for "There won't be a need to call many penalties on us."

STORMY, THEN STEADY

Once his team returned to the locker room, the composed Scifres gathered his players around.

He had remained calm and controlled all day. He began his pregame speech much the same way. By the end, however, his face was red, his words sharp, his voice rising to a level players seldom hear.

"Seniors, it was your destiny to be here right now! At this point, you have to make your destiny. Do you have the character, the heart? Do you have the faith in God? Do you have the courage every play, to step up like a man?"

With that, Scifres brought his team in tight for a final prayer.

"I want you all to know how much I love you," he said before leading the team through the tunnel and back onto the field to play its biggest game of the year.

The Rebels responded by fumbling the ball on the first play of the game.

Scifres showed no emotion.

The Rebels fell behind 10–0 in the first quarter then responded by going up 14–10 at the half.

Scifres' expression never changed.

At halftime, Scifres stopped to do a television interview and then returned to the locker room. He and the coaches convened for ten minutes in a small room and quietly discussed adjustments.

Scifres then met briefly with his players. Again, the fire was back, but temporarily.

"We're exactly where we want to be," he said. "Win this half and you win a state championship!"

He would show no emotion again until senior Phil Andrews pulled in quarterback Andrew Hasty's third touchdown pass of the game, and the Rebels took a decisive 35–10 lead. He offered a quick pump of his arm and then a lengthier hug to Andrews, whose father, Karl Andrews, had died in summer of 2002.

"You know your dad was there with you," Scifres said to Andrews.

"Coach Scifres is not only a coach, he's more like a father figure to all of us," Andrews would say later.

The run-oriented Rebels shocked the Warriors with a season-high 215 yards passing.

"He is very open to tailoring our talent to an offense . . . to let kids be able to do what they can do," Puntarelli said. "Especially the last few years, I think he's done a great job with that."

POSTGAME CELEBRATION

As the seconds ticked off and players began celebrating, Scifres walked slowly across the field to shake Rietveld's hand. He met with the media and did many interviews on the field.

The Rebels had been state champions for nearly a half-hour, and Scifres had yet to find time to celebrate himself.

Finally, he found his two sons, who had served as water boys, and kissed their heads. He walked over to the stands and found his family, including his mother, who leaned over to receive her son's kiss.

He returned to the field to be photographed, do more interviews and hug players and coaches. As the field cleared, Scifres looked around.

"Is there anyone I haven't hugged yet?"

The loudest ovation at the dome was reserved for Scifres when he received his blue ribbon as his name was being announced.

He walked off the field, clutching a game ball in one hand and his playbook in the other. Chants of "Bruuuucce" rang down from the stands. He smiled and waved the red binder in the direction of the fans.

In the locker room, cleanup was swift. Players gathered their gear and returned to the buses. There was no post-game speech. Scifres hugged a few of the seniors as they made their way out of the locker room. Hasty was the last player remaining, sitting alone and crying. Scifres put his arms around his senior quarterback and quietly said the right words. Hasty smiled, wiped back his tears of joy and made his way to the bus.

"You really become close with them," Scifres said. "We hope when they come out of our program, we've been able to instill lifetime lessons, lessons these kids will take with them the rest of their lives. Through all of that, in many respects, they become like my sons."

As the bus pulled up at the high school, the players and coaches began singing the school song, with Scifres sitting in the front seat and leading the chorus, pumping his arms. He still clutched the worn-out, red playbook, which would soon finally get a break of its own.

I was very thankful to Paul Shepherd who wrote this article. It was a well written summary of the day and a wonderful tribute to our program. The article helped reinforce in my mind the concept that this group truly was a "Team of Destiny." Moreover, it underscored how blessed I was to be a part of it all!

What happened was meant to be. I couldn't have scripted it any better.

CHAPTER 14

The Keys To Success

We made history. By winning the 2004 State Championship, our program obtained some "firsts" in Indiana high school football:

> ❧ We were the first team in Indiana 4A football to win three consecutive state championships. Again, this occurred after we had been bumped from 3A football in 2001 — with many people saying we would struggle to compete in the larger class.

> ❧ More significantly, we became the first team in Indiana history to win eight Football State Championships.

> ❧ Finally, I became the first head football coach from Indiana to win six state titles in a twelve year time span.

Combined with the fact that I was the head track coach of a State Runner-Up team in 1990, I have enjoyed my fair share of success as a high school coach. I have truly been blessed.

Periodically, I am asked what are the keys to our success? Typically, I break them down into two categories. The first is what I call "the mechanics of success." These are the physical activities to get you where you want to be, including working hard, being loyal and dependable for others, and setting goals to serve as a road map for achievement. Although these are all important to attain success, I believe the second category, which tends to be more philosophical, leads to greater accomplishments and certainly a more fulfilling life.

I don't believe being successful necessarily equates to wealth or social status. To the contrary, I think everyone knows people who are wealthy and have many material possessions but are really unhappy in their personal life. Interestingly, studies have shown that suicide rates are highest around the world in wealthy countries and occur most commonly in families of reasonable affluence. Being wealthy has little to do with contentment or joy. Therefore, it must not be the key to success.

In this philosophical approach towards happiness, we must first take stock of ourselves and our relationships with others. How do we treat those whose lives we come in contact with each day? I believe our actions have a "mirror effect" — meaning the image we present to others will usually be reflected right back at us. Likewise, the words we choose to use with others have the same result as shouting into a cave — good or bad, they will come echoing right back at us. I have grown to believe this is a fundamental weakness that has developed in our society today. It is so easy to point the finger of blame at others for our lot in life. Yet, we often fail to recognize that we are primarily responsible for our own happiness.

Consider for a moment that over half of all marriages in America end in divorce. Then consider that in many parts of provincial China, it is customary for a man and woman who are considering divorce to stand in front of a committee to publicly share the problems their marriage is facing. However, before they can say anything negative against their spouse, they must first spend twenty minutes discussing their own faults, shortcomings, personality flaws and ways they have contributed to the dissolution of the marriage. Needless to say, the Chinese experience only a fraction of the divorces we have in this country. I believe our society would be well-served to have this kind of self-examination and personal accountability. I also contend that an honest and thorough self-assessment is the first step in leading to a happier, more fulfilled life.

The second step towards success is to periodically take a few moments to realize the many blessings we all have in our lives. I am reminded of "The World's Funniest Joke." At the start of the twenty-first century, thousands of people around the world were polled to determine what joke would be deemed most humorous. The following was the favorite:

> *Sherlock Holmes and his trusty assistant, Dr. Watson, were on a camping trip. In the middle of the night, Sherlock awoke and immediately took notice of the billions of brightly lit stars in the sky. He nudged his friend, who was sound asleep, and said, "Watson, I want you to look up at all the stars in the sky and tell me what you deduce from what you see." Watson, who was well aware of his friend's uncanny ability to trick him with these types of questions, was determined not to let it happen again. After pondering for a few moments, he replied, "Well, Sherlock, I recall from my background in astronomy that each of those stars in the sky are actually suns — very much like our own. As such, it is highly likely that many of them have planets revolving around them, as in our own solar system. Consequently, I would deduce that somewhere in the universe there is a planet very similar to Earth and that there is, indeed, life elsewhere in the universe." Watson was confident that he nailed it. With a smug look on his face, he asked, "Well, Sherlock, how did I do?" Sherlock replied, with a rather disgusted tone to his voice, "Well, Watson, you nitwit! You were supposed to deduce that someone has stolen our tent!"*

Although I know I've heard funnier jokes over the years, I think there's an important message we can take from poor Dr. Watson's ill-fated deduction. How many times in our lives do we fail to see what is right in front of us because we are so intent on gazing at the stars beyond? How often do we take our families and loved ones for granted while we are in pursuit of a higher salary, a new car or a bigger home?

An interesting perspective on this is to imagine how desperate you would immediately become if you were suddenly approached on the street by someone who took your keys and wallet away. Imagine how you would feel if you were told you would never see your family, your home or your vehicle again, and that you were destined to live the rest of your life on the street with none of those comforts. After two weeks on the street, imagine how ecstatic you would be if that same person gave back your keys and wallet, and said your family and friends were waiting at home for your arrival and your life would return to normal.

I'm sure this exercise would help each of us realize just how blessed we truly are. Realizing and being thankful for our many blessings is the second step toward happiness and success in life.

Several things deserve mention in connection with the blessings that resulted from the 2004 season. Several of our players received recognition on honor teams. Five players were named 1st Team All-State: Casey Bolsega (offensive tackle), Billy Cobb (linebacker), Taylor Donnel (tight end), Pat Kuntz (defensive end) and Jason Werner (defensive back.) Just as impressively, we had fourteen players named to the Academic All-State Team, which was the most ever from our school.

Earlier, I mentioned that Roncalli had gone twenty years since a football player was last offered a scholarship to a Big Ten school. This senior class had three! In spite of the fact that he missed his senior season with a knee surgery, Indiana University offered Tim Sergi a full ride. I have absolutely no doubt this was a wise decision on their part. Purdue University made an offer to Jason Werner which he accepted. Finally, Pat Kuntz had offers from several Big Ten schools but ultimately signed with Notre Dame. I believe all three will have great collegiate careers.

Jason had a storybook season. Through the six games of the state tournament, he had nine interceptions, caught touchdown passes, threw a touchdown pass, blocked a PAT (in a game we won by 1 point), ran for the winning touchdown in the closing minutes of two games and ended three consecutive games with interceptions in the last minute of play to preserve narrow leads. After being selected as Indiana's Best High School Football Player by coaches and media around the state, he was presented with the Indianapolis Star "Mr. Football Award." In reality, despite the accolades and awards, his character, work ethic, friendly demeanor and humble approach to life make him an even better person than football player.

Andrew Hasty also played the game of his life in the state finals. He passed for 215 yards and his 3 touchdown passes tied Jeff George for the most touchdowns thrown in a 4A state game. George was an outstanding Indiana high school football player, who has also had a long and storied career as an NFL quarterback. Who would have predicted this considering Roncalli's run-oriented offense?

Likewise, no one would have predicted that Scott Lutgring (all 5' 9", 170 lbs. of him) would rush for over 1,800 yards, score 25 touchdowns and, at times, carry the team on his back to a third consecutive state championship. For the rest of my career I will use him as an example of what can happen when you commit yourself to a cause, stay focused and work tirelessly to achieve your goals. He was more than deserving of the success he enjoyed.

Finally, I will never forget the lessons I learned from Nate Ashworth and Tim Sergi. Certainly, the old adage "Adversity does not build character, it reveals it" applies to both of these young men. The determination each of them demonstrated in overcoming heartbreak and misfortune was amazing. Even more remarkable was their ability to maintain positive leadership skills and great attitudes through it all. The last award I announce at our post-season football awards banquet is the Mental Attitude Award. During our 2004 gathering, I announced that from that moment on, the award would be called the Nate Ashworth

Mental Attitude Award. After calling Nate up to receive his plaque, I asked if he would present another plaque to the first recipient of the award given in his name. I then announced Tim Sergi as the winner. As they stood at the front of the room, everyone in attendance gave them a long and much deserved standing ovation. I'll never forget the lessons these young men taught all of us that season. These are just a few of the many blessings from the 2004 season.

In addition to taking an honest account of ourselves and realizing the countless ways our lives have been blessed, the third key to success is to find happiness and contentment in our daily routine. Henry David Thoreau's words "most men lead lives of quiet desperation" have never rung more true than they do today. So many people, both male and female, go through their lives lacking a real sense of purpose. Consequently, their existence seems to lack meaning.

Recently, I read an article about the "Top Ten" things that lead to happiness in a person's job. The results were interesting. The number one item was not salary, benefits or a new company car. Surprisingly, the top factor was having a job where workers felt they were helping others. Reading this made me smile and it also helped me understand why I love my job as a teacher and coach. I am a firm believer in the phrase, "We are God's hands." When we do things for other people, they see God through us. Ultimately, this adds value and meaning to our lives, and can be an ongoing source of gratification and happiness.

There's another saying I've always liked, "Preach the gospel at all times. When necessary ... use words." I hope the young people I come in contact with at Roncalli see Christ through my actions each day. Often times, I see Christ through them. This is truly what makes Roncalli such a special place and leads to great job satisfaction for me.

I realize many careers are not as conducive to helping others as is teaching. However, regardless of a person's career, individuals can always find ways of helping others — through volunteer work and generosity. I believe helping others is a huge step towards happiness and ultimate success in life.

The fourth key to success is realizing that our lives are filled with choices. Each day we must choose our attitude because this truly is the only thing in life over which we have complete control. We must decide how we are going to treat those around us and how we are going to respond to the way others treat us. Each day we choose who to love and who to separate from that love. And finally, we choose whether or not we are going to be happy. Without question, happiness is a choice. Eleanor Roosevelt once said, "No one can make me feel inferior without my consent!" I contend that no one can make me unhappy without my consent.

For most of my life, I have chosen to be happy. Although we didn't have much money in a family of eight kids, I have fond memories of growing up. I had a happy childhood and just knowing my mom and dad loved me was a huge part of that. Continuing to teach at a parochial school has ensured that my own family will never have a lot of money but I think we all live pretty happy lives. I love my wife, my children, my family, my God and I love the young men I coach and what I do for a living. For those reasons, I consider myself to be one of the wealthiest men I know and ultimately these are choices I make every day. Choosing to be happy is one of the most important elements of success.

Just like we remind our players as they leave the locker room before a game, the fifth and final key to success is to "Take God with you on every play." This, too, is our choice. We decide every day whether or not we pray and, likewise, we choose to what degree we allow God into our hearts to guide us. Clinical studies have proven the merits of prayer. Researchers have found that regular prayer helps reduce anxiety and depression, and also works to boost self-esteem.

I firmly believe that faith and prayer are at the core of true happiness. As I reflect on the stages of my life when I allowed myself to grow distant from God, without question those were the times when I felt a void in my heart and a lack of purpose in my life.

As I have learned to fill that void with God's love, every aspect of my life becomes more fulfilling; personally, professionally and spiritually. Consequently, this is what I want to share with the young men I coach. Far beyond teaching them how to block and tackle, these lessons change their lives. At this stage in my career, these "victories" have become far more gratifying than those that take place on the gridiron. The act of doing God's work to help others creates real happiness, and therein lies true success.

In summary, I'd like to restate the words of Tony Dungy, "Commit everything you do to the Lord, and you will be successful." I have never heard a more accurate "Key to Success!"

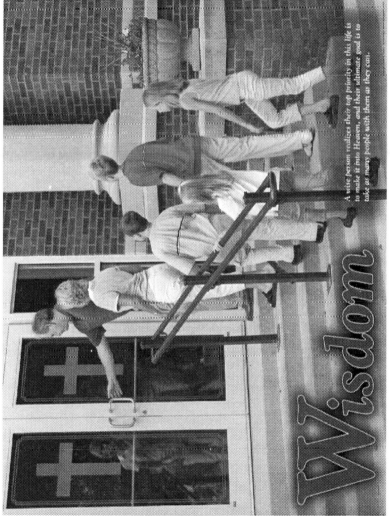

A wise person realizes their top priority in this life is to make it into Heaven, and their ultimate goal is to take as many people with them as they can.

Wisdom

193

CHAPTER 15

Seeking the Wall

There's yardage beyond the goal line. I have grown to believe it is my responsibility as a teacher and coach to assist in three primary areas of growth for the young people with whom I work. These are physical, mental and spiritual development. I rank them in this order because I feel this coincides with the hierarchy of importance of these qualities in regard to success throughout one's lifetime. Let me explain. I have developed what I call the "Scifres Philosophy of Success."

Having been an educator for twenty-five years, it is apparent that early success in school (commonly equated to popularity) is almost always related to a person's physical attributes. Through grade school and even into high school, the most successful (popular) kids are nearly always the best looking or the most athletically and physically talented students. The smartest or most sweet-natured kids are rarely the most popular. This leads to a constant struggle to "fit in" with the popular group. Those who have received the least amount of physical gifts are usually the ones who struggle most. Sometimes this interaction can be quite cruel.

As a person enters college, the physically gifted still have some advantages. However, success begins to balance out with those who possess more intellectual gifts. Upon entering the work force after graduation, one's mental abilities and academic preparation tend to determine the job you land and ultimately the house you live in and the car you drive. Doctors, lawyers, architects, etc. don't need to be either good looking or athletic. Until a person reaches retirement, success in the "middle stage" of life is primarily dependent on mental abilities.

My contention is that, in the final stages of our life, ultimate success is based on where we stand in our spiritual development. How many touchdowns we scored or how many homeruns we hit in Little League baseball will be irrelevant. Who made the cheerleading squad or who was voted Homecoming Queen will not matter. Likewise, our savings account or the size of home we occupied will pale in comparison to how we chose to live our life, what we did with the gifts God gave us and the impact we made on the lives of those we came into contact with each day. As a middle-aged man, this "philosophy" has really struck home with me.

I truly believe God has given me a wonderful gift by allowing me to teach and coach. It is my responsibility to work towards the physical, mental and spiritual development of the young people put in my charge - particularly in working with our players. I have a daily opportunity to teach them about what it means to be a "Real Man." In my role as a coach, I am able to teach a "code of conduct" for manhood. I want all of our players to love and honor their parents, and to eventually become faithful husbands and loving fathers to their children. Through my example, I want them to see that it is okay to look another male in the eyes and say "I love you" or "I am very proud of you!" I want them to realize their success as a man doesn't depend on what they own, but should be measured instead in terms of their capacity to love and be loved. I want to teach them there is a purpose for their existence in this world and that God had something very special in mind when He created each of them. When they begin to realize this, I believe they will become more inclined to love and serve Him in return.

With each of our players, I have the unique opportunity to nourish the seed of God's love in their soul. During their four years with us, it is my duty to nurture that seed so it might eventually grow and bear fruit, creating a better understanding of the depth of God's love for each of us and an increased desire to follow in the footsteps of Jesus.

As a ball carrier in high school and college, it was my life ambition to cross the goal line as many times as possible with the football in my hands. Certainly, this is the premise of the game. But what I have grown to love and respect most about football is that there is, in fact, yardage beyond the goal line. It is more than scoring touchdowns. The lessons learned about hard work, determination, loyalty, sacrifice, mental tenacity and a better understanding of the depths of brotherly love are life-changing.

Long after our players have forgotten how to block the 50 Defense and their bodies are too sore to run and tackle, I hope they will all understand the best measure of a man's greatness is how he influences and impacts other people's lives. It is through these lessons that they learn to become a man. In turn, they will have the opportunity and duty to pass these lessons on to their children. Frequently, I have thought that the true results of my coaching and the kind of job I did as a mentor may not be evident for many years to come. I have learned not to measure my success as a coach with win-loss records, rings, trophies or championsips. As long as my focus each year is on turning a group of boys into a group of solid Christian young men, I will never have a losing season!

Since making "The Covenant" with God prior to the 1999 season, I have often reflected on the price I have paid as a coach compared to the benefits I have received in return. Like all coaches, I have given a lot of time and energy in an effort to help parents raise their children. Most notably, in the fall, I give up a lot of sleep. This is chiefly a self-imposed misery, which I continually try to improve. The last thing I have given a lot of is prayer. I continue to pray for our players and their families even after they have graduated. Of course, I always pray for strength and wisdom to perform my job in a way that is appealing to God.

It is in my spiritual life that I have grown to appreciate the many blessings I have received. There is a correlation between committing myself to do this work and the peace and contentment I have known in my personal life. My blessings center around my beautiful wife and my four precious children. As a young man, I used to dream that one day I would meet someone with whom I would fall in love and in return, their love for me would make my life complete. That dream came true. I want to make sure Jackie knows each day how much I love and respect her and our children. They truly are gifts from God!

Professionally, my life has been blessed as well. In the past six years, we have won four state championships. Far more meaningful than the victories, however, has been the interaction with the young men I have coached. As their coach, I am supposed to educate them about football and life. What I have found is the harder I work at teaching life lessons, the more I learn from them. Likewise, the more I give to them, the more I get in return. Helping them develop their faith and then being able to observe them witness their beliefs as they lead team prayer or Senior Scripture has been immensely rewarding. Seeing the faith and courage of Marcus Nalley, Jonathan Page, Phil Andrews, Nate Ashworth and Tim Sergi has been tremendously inspirational. I am fortunate to have been a part of their lives.

When our 2004 State Championship rings arrived, we had a wonderful dinner for our players and their families. After dinner, we distributed the rings and championship plaques to the players and coaches. When this was complete, the seniors said they had a presentation to make. We watched as they carried in beautiful mailboxes that had been customized and decorated for each coach. Mine had been meticulously created by John Conover, a Roncalli alum and the father of two former players. Inside each mailbox were letters written to the coaches from the players.

When I returned home, my son, Luke, was sitting in the family room watching TV. I sat down with my mailbox and be-

gan to read my first letter. About three sentences into it, I had to
leave the room. Luke has never seen me cry and I knew my
emotions would take over and make tears inevitable. The letters
were filled with words of love, respect, gratitude and admiration. Each one touched my soul in a way that a larger paycheck,
a bigger home or a nicer car never could. In my heart, these
letters also reinforced how lucky I am to coach the young men I
do and that I'm teaching at exactly the school where God wants
me to be. I've received many wonderful gifts in my years as a
coach, but these letters are now among my most prized possessions. I will keep them always, lest I ever question what it is I'm
doing with my life.

I entitled this book "Beyond the Goal Line, the Quest For
Victory in the Game of Life." As I've reflected on my journey
with God, I have often asked myself, "Where do I find meaning
and purpose in my life?" I think it's good to periodically take
account of where our priorities lie. Where is our time and energy spent? What "Wall of Fame" are we striving to have our
name etched upon when our life on Earth ends? Would it be the
golf Wall of Fame? Or, perhaps, it might be the "Top Salesman"
or "Top Wage Earner" or maybe the hardest worker with the
most hours spent. Often times, I question myself about this during football season. To what Wall of Fame am I dedicating my
life?

A couple of years ago, I was contemplating this thought
and wrote the following poem:

Heaven's Wall

As we live our life on Earth
What do we hope to gain?
Is it power that we seek
Or is it wealth or fame?

Are we busy building up
Possessions here on Earth
Do we use the things we own

To measure our true worth?

Or are we more concerned with how
We treat our fellow man
Knowing that the Golden Rule
Follows God's master plan?

And if we choose to steer our lives
Along Christ Jesus' path
He will be the author of
Our celestial epitaph.

So when we stand at Heaven's gates
We'll look and find our name
Shining brightly and inscribed
On Heaven's Wall of Fame.

I believe there will come a day when I will be held accountable for the gifts God has given me, how I chose to use those gifts and, ultimately, the influence I had on others. I want to live my life with purpose; I want my journey to matter; I want to make a difference for those whose lives I touch. I do want to make it to Heaven and, along the way, I want to bring as many people with me as I can.

This is the yardage beyond the goal line!

I pray that if I work hard, do my best to live my life according to the example set by Jesus and, in the process, strive to get others to do the same, I might someday find my name etched in a place of honor on Heaven's Wall of Fame. I now realize this is the wall I am seeking.

Since forming my covenant with God, my hope is to someday hear him say, "Job well done, my good and faithful servant." I can only imagine the pride, joy and honor that will fill my heart. I will know I have completed my last contest and have won the ultimate championship ...

I will have claimed victory in the game of life.

HEAVEN'S WALL

As we live our life on earth
What do we hope to gain,
Is it power that we seek
Or is it wealth and fame?

Are we busy building up
Possessions here on earth
Do we use the things we own
To measure our true worth?

Or are we more concerned with how
We treat our fellow man
Knowing that the golden rule
Follows God's master plan?

And if we choose to steer our lives
Along Christ Jesus' path
He will be the author of
Our celestial epitaph.

So when we stand at Heaven's gates
We'll look and find our name
Shining brightly and inscribed
On Heaven's Wall of Fame.

Inspirational Posters

Over the years I have worked on inspirational sayings, poems and posters as a form of motivation for our athletes. Most of them blend an element of spirituality with an athletic message. Some are strictly faith-based and are not necessarily associated with athletics. Each poster is 18" X 24" with a nice finish. These make wonderful gifts, as they serve as daily reminders of God's love for us.

We have created a web-site from which these posters can be ordered. Additional copies of this book can also be ordered from this web-site. The payment plan is through Pay Pal, one of the most secure payment programs on the internet. You can order with complete confidence in security through Pay Pal! Every poster included with this book is protected under copyright law, all rights reserved.

Please visit our web-site at: *www.inspireposters.com*

Thank you for reading this book. May God bless you and those you love!

Sincerely,

Bruce Scipres

Thank you, Lord, for the opportunity
    You have given me this day,
To use my gifts to participate in
    This sport I love to play.

Thank you for my loved ones, Lord,
    Who came to watch this game.
Help me to bring pride and honor
    To my family name.

Help me to remember, Lord,
    As I begin to tire,
As fatigue starts to run it's course
    To keep that competitive fire.

For no amount of stress or pain
    That I might feel today,
Can match what Jesus sacrificed
    When crucified that day.

Please grant me strength and courage
    To compete with a warrior's heart,
To be a champion in your eyes
    And finish what I start.

So that when this day is done
    And I lay down to rest,
I will know deep in my heart
    That I have done my best.

An Athlete's Prayer

I Can Do All Things Through Him Who Strengthens Me.
Phil. 4:13

Actual size 18" x 24"

An Athlete's Prayer is designed to inspire athletes of all ages. This poster is available with all the sports listed on this page. Pick and choose your favorite!

Boy's Football

Girl's Volleyball

Girl's Soccer

Girl's Basketball

Boy's Soccer

Boy's Basketball

Girl's Softball

Boy's Baseball

A Role Model

An Athlete's Responsibility

*To the world you may mean very little,
but to someone little you may mean the world.*

Actual size 18" x 24"

A Real Coach

A REAL COACH knows that his primary responsibility is not to teach the mechanics of his sport, but rather the fundamentals of life. He prioritizes sportsmanship, and teaches his athletes to maintain integrity and class in victory or defeat. He instills honesty and a sense of fair play. His athletes learn the merits of hard work and enthusiasm as they observe him model these traits each day. He teaches them to be thankful for their abilities and to always do their best to utilize their gifts. His athletes learn to never give up in the face of adversity, and that their attitude is the only thing in life over which they have complete control.

A REAL COACH knows that his ultimate goal is not to win championships or individual accolades. Instead, it is to teach a boy to become a man. He understands the only scoreboard that really matters is the one in his heart. For it is here that he sees the score that counts most... HOW MANY LIVES HE HAS TOUCHED AND CHANGED FOR THE BETTER. This is where a REAL COACH finds his greatest reward.

(Available in female tense)

Actual size 18" x 24"

Actual size 18" x 24"

Grace

All of this . . . because of his love for me.

Actual size 18" x 24"

Success

Success in this life is not measured by what you own,
but rather how much you are loved by your own.

Heaven's Wall

As we live our life on earth
  What do we hope to gain,
Is it power that we seek
  Or is it wealth and fame?

Are we busy building up
  Possessions here on earth
Do we use the things we own
  To measure our true worth?

Or are we more concerned with how
  We treat our fellow man
Knowing that the golden rule
  Follows God's master plan?

And if we choose to steer our lives
  Along Christ Jesus' path
He will be the author of
  Our celestial epitaph.

So when we stand at Heaven's gates
  We'll look and find our name
Shining brightly and inscribed
  On Heaven's Wall of Fame.

Wisdom

A wise person realizes their top priority in this life is to make it into Heaven, and their ultimate goal is to take as many people with them as they can.

Actual size 24" x 18"

Actual size 24" x 18"

Customized Poster

11" x 14"

With the power of technology, Inspireposters© can even create our posters with your customized image. Email us a picture of the athlete or coach you want imposed and we will do the rest. Visit our web site for more details. These make great personalized gifts for your family and loved ones by uplifting those that inspire you.

A Real Coach

A REAL COACH knows that the primary responsibility is not to teach the mechanics of his sport, but rather the fundamentals of life. He prepares sportsmanship and teaches his athletes to maintain integrity and class in victory or defeat. He instills honesty and a sense of fair play. His athletes learn the merits of hard work and enthusiasm as they observe him model these traits each day. He teaches them to be thankful for their abilities and to always do their best to utilize their gifts. His athletes learn to never give up in the face of adversity, and their best attitude is put only deep in his love which they have come control.

A REAL COACH knows that his ultimate goal is not to win championships or individual accolades. Instead, it is to teach a boy to become a man. He understands the only scoreboard that really matters is the one in his heart. For it is here that he sees the score that counts most... HOW MANY LIVES HE HAS TOUCHED AND CHANGED FOR THE BETTER. This is where A REAL COACH finds his greatest reward.

Actual size 11" x 14"

An Athlete's Prayer

I Can Do All Things Through Him Who Str...

Phil. 4:13

Actual size 11" x 14"